Old Bridge … d Blairlogie

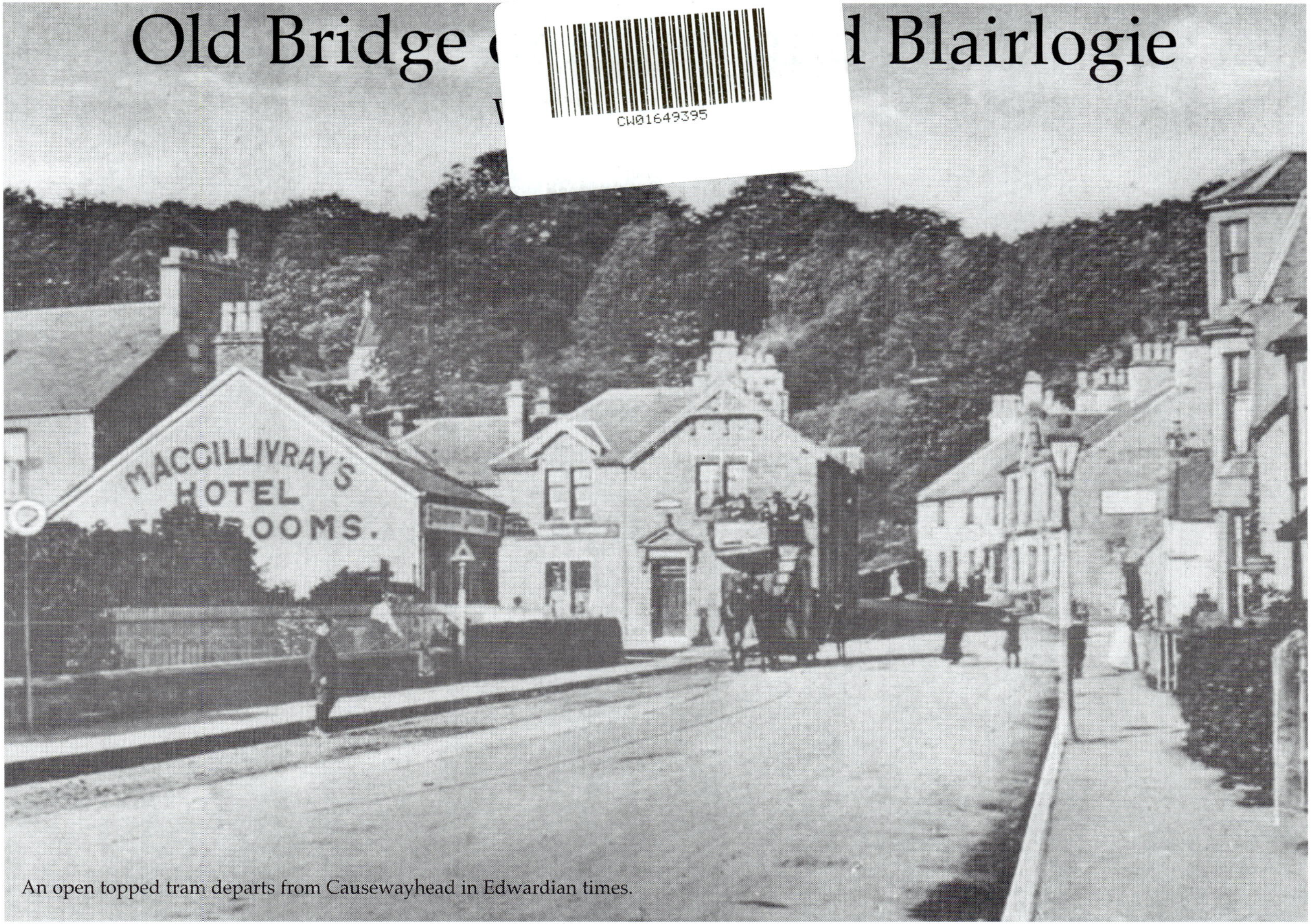

An open topped tram departs from Causewayhead in Edwardian times.

First Published in the United Kingdom, 2007
Stenlake Publishing Limited
54–58 Mill Square, Catrine, KA5 6RD
www.stenlake.co.uk

ISBN 9781840333879

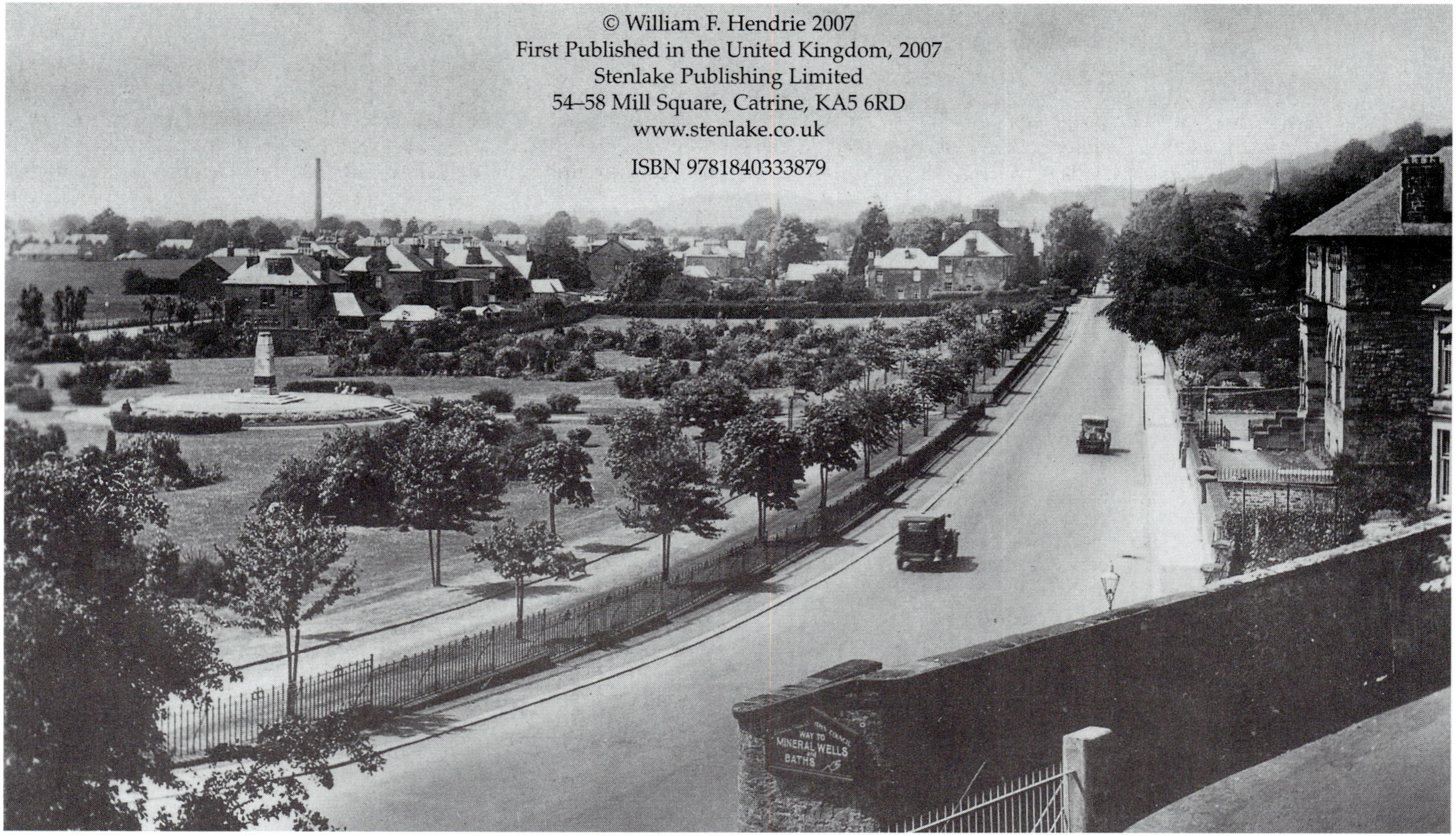

This panoramic shot looks out over the spacious Pullar Memorial Gardens, gifted to the town by John Pullar, Provost from 1870 to 1873, whose family owned the Bleach Works. On the right is the Museum Hall, built to house the McFarlane Collection amassed by John McFarlane who lived at Coneyhill House, which later became the Old Manor Hotel and is now a private residence again. McFarlane was the uncle of Sir John Murray, the pioneering oceanographer who gained great fame as the director of the famous Challenger expedition. Murray did much work on his uncle's scientific collection, which on the closure of the museum was transferred to the Smith Museum in Stirling. For many years the hall continued to stage musical and theatrical performances, but has lain unused since 1978. In December 2006 it was sold to a property developer, who it is understood will construct flats behind the old facade.

INTRODUCTION

"A really delightful place" was how Dorothy Wordsworth described Bridge of Allan, when she toured Scotland with her famous brother, the poet William Wordsworth. A century and a half later her words equally well sum up what has become one of Stirling's most attractive suburbs. Nearby to the east, Bridge of Allan's neighbour, Blairlogie, has seen far less development and retains its original village character.

Bridge of Allan owes its origins to travellers who originally forded the River Allan here, three miles to the north west of Stirling, on journeys to Perth, Inverness and the Highlands. In those days there were two separate small communities here on opposite banks of the river - Inverallan to the west and Pathfoot to the east. In 1520 the often dangerous crossing was made much safer by the construction of a stone bridge. The brig gave us our name, as the local inhabitants aptly put it, and Bridge of Allan became recognised as one village.

Throughout the 17th and 18th centuries Bridge of Allan developed slowly. Work was provided by its meal mill, whose water wheel was powered by a lade from the river and a copper mine on the steep hillside which rose behind its huddle of cottages. When the mine ceased production in 1807, the future of the village looked unpromising, but soon afterwards prospects suddenly changed for the better. Analysis of the water which had flooded the disused mine workings revealed that it had a high salt content, an attribute much sought after by the Victorians because of its laxative powers, which subsequently they convinced themselves were health giving.

As a result Bridge of Allan was reborn as one of Scotland's most successful spa towns and grew into a flourishing inland holiday resort. The heart of the village was transformed into a model town, with its main thoroughfare named after its designer, Major John Henderson. Both sides of broad imposing Henderson Street were lined with impressive stone built hotels and what were described as rooming houses where self-catering accommodation could be rented by the week or the month by those who arrived to take the waters.

By 1830 a description of Bridge of Allan stated that it was "everything a village ought to be with its straw roofed cottages, a mill, old inns with entertainment for man and horse and a row of neat little villas for the fashionable who flood to it in summer".

To begin with the holidaymakers arrived by coach or aboard the horse-drawn omnibus which plied five times a day between Stirling and Bridge of Allan. The arrival of the railway in 1848, only six years after the opening of Scotland's first passenger route between Edinburgh and Glasgow, brought even more visitors. The arrival of each steam train was met by a fleet of horse-drawn buses, which waited outside the brick-built station in Station Road to convey the travellers and their piles of heavy luggage to the various hotels and boarding houses. The most posh was the Royal Hotel, that belonged to Mr. Philps and was vividly painted in a tartan pattern. Bridge of Allan Station became such a busy place that John Menzies opened one of his first newsagents and bookstalls on its platform.

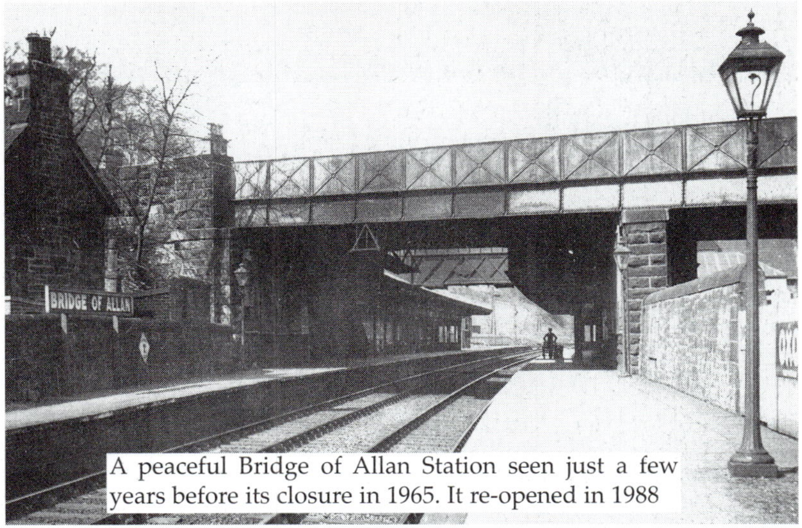

A peaceful Bridge of Allan Station seen just a few years before its closure in 1965. It re-opened in 1988

Queen Victoria paid the growing spa town a royal visit and amongst other well-known visitors were Charles Dickens, the Wordsworths and the Stevenson family of lighthouse building fame, who brought their young son Robert Louis there on many occasions following his first visit at the age of two. The boy's imagination was fired by his discovery that there was a cave on the banks of the Allan. To reach the cave, Louis followed what is now known as the Allan or Darn Walk. Later in his writings he noted that he would never forget his days at Bridge of Allan, they were one golden dream. He also noted that his favourite walk was by the riverside among the pines and the ash trees. His observation that "There is a little cavern here which has been a part of me these last twelve years or more" has often led Bridge of Allan's inhabitants to claim that it was while holidaying there that he got the inspiration for the cave which castaway Ben Gunn occupied in his classic children's adventure novel, Treasure Island.

Apart from the delights of riverside rambles and walking in the hills, Bridge of Allan catered well for its guests, fully occupying their leisure hours by offering a selection of sports including fly fishing (for trout), golf and tennis. The Scottish Lawn Tennis Championship was held in Bridge of Allan on several occasions. Winter frosts brought the excitement of trying curling and the thrills of ice skating on frozen ponds, some lit with lanterns so that the fun could continue after dark and late into the night.

Bridge of Allan was recognised as a burgh with its own town council in 1870, a status which it proudly retained until Lord Wheatley's reform of Scottish local government in 1975. As befitted such a flourishing 19th century spa resort, Bridge of Allan gained its own large hydropathic hotel in 1864. Fit to rival its neighbour in nearby Dunblane, the Ochilpark Hydro was built high on the hillside above the town and for guests intent on pursuing water cures offered the services of its own resident physician and masseur. In 1893 the Hydro changed its name to the Allan Water Hotel, but remained as luxurious as before.

By the1890s travel between Bridge of Allan and Stirling had been made even easier by the construction of a single track tram line with open top horse-drawn carriages, which operated from 1870 until 1920, when plans to electrify it were abandoned in the face of competition from motor buses. The service provided by the buses was more flexible and instead of expanding, the tramway subsequently closed.

For over a century Bridge of Allan's important holiday trade succeeded in coexisting with the town's other small industries, including its paper mill powered by the Allan Water and the bleach works which was also on its banks. The bleach works was owned by the famous Pullar family of Perth who, typical of many employers of their age exercised a paternalistic interest in the well-being of their employees and built a workmens' institute and reading room at the entrance to the works.

Despite the existence of these industries within its boundaries, during the Second World War Bridge of Allan was looked upon as sufficiently safe to receive evacuated children from Glasgow, even though there were army camps sited around the town while the requisitioned Royal Hotel accommodated officers. Later in the war many Polish troops were billeted in the town and impressed the local women with their smart uniforms, the clicking of their heels and their continental charm and good manners. Many of these foreign servicemen received hospitality from local families although rationing was restricting the availability of food in the grocers and butchers shops of Henderson Street and Fountain Street. Following the return of peace in 1945, post-war austerity affected the town badly. The Allan Water Hotel reopened in 1946 but failed to flourish and eventually closed. It and several of the town's large private villas have been converted into flats.

The acquisition in 1967 of the Airthrey Estate on the eastern edge of Bridge of Allan as the site for

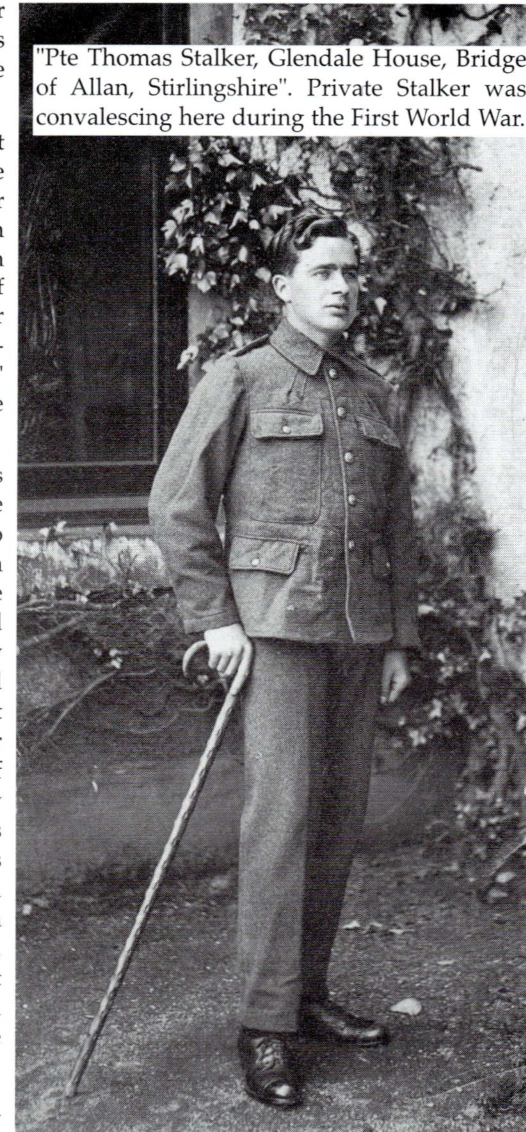
"Pte Thomas Stalker, Glendale House, Bridge of Allan, Stirlingshire". Private Stalker was convalescing here during the First World War.

the new University of Stirling, however, did much to revive the local economy as members of faculty and students alike soon recognised it as the ideal place to live. The attractive and spacious campus of the university sited around Airthrey Loch provides residents of Bridge of Allan with a wide range of attractions in which they are encouraged to participate from its excellent library to its 500 seat theatre and cinema in the MacRobert Centre, named after its most famous benefactor.

The town benefited still further as a place to stay or visit when in the early 1970s it was bypassed by the M9. The northern section of the motorway was completed first, in 1971, with the southern section opened two years later. The removal of heavy vehicles from its main street made Bridge of Allan all the more pleasant a place in which to live, shop and explore.

Dorothy Wordsworth qualified her "a most delightful place" compliment by going on to declare, "but it amuses one how difficult it is to understand the Scotch. They can't make out what I am saying either. I was talking to an old man and he had to fetch his daughter to interpret. It's like being in a foreign country". Such a comment is no longer applicable, because thanks to the influence of the university and its range of attractive houses, this Stirling suburb has grown into one of Scotland's liveliest international communities.

Blairlogie on the other hand has been bypassed by most of these changes. Nestling almost hidden at the foot of the impressive Ochil Hills, Blairlogie is the first of the Hillfoot Villages driving east from Stirling and, thanks to its setting, remains almost entirely free of traffic. For this reason it is little known to any apart from its residents, who rather like to keep it so.

For the curious, Blairlogie is well worth discovering because with its crow step gables, red pantiled roofs and traditional fore stairs outside many of its cottage homes, it is a true gem of a village. Overlooked by Blairlogie Castle, a small 16th century tower house, the buildings in Blairlogie boast many features of architectural interest, from the 18th century kirk to the row of cottages which have now been converted into a modern village hall.

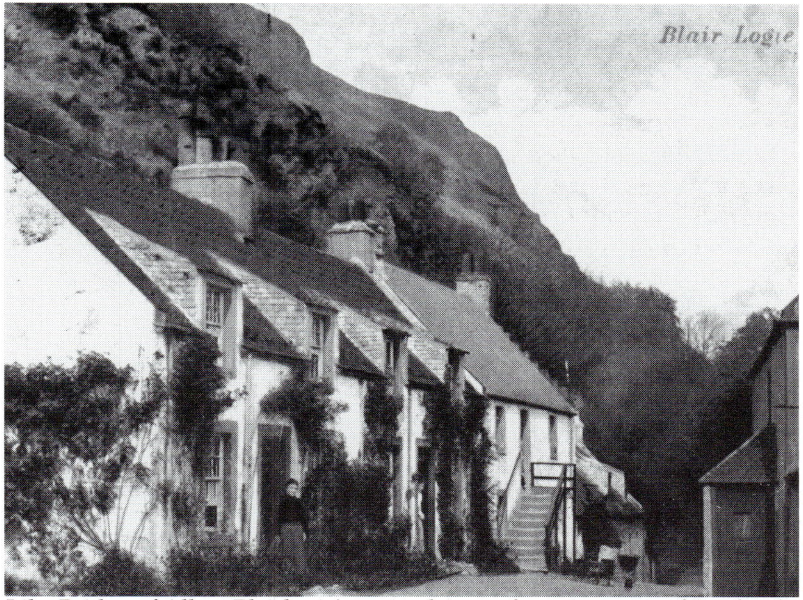

Like Bridge of Allan, Blairlogie's main claim to fame is as one of Scotland's Victorian spa towns. In the case of Blairlogie it was not pure clear water that brought health seeking visitors to it, but the availability of milk from its large herd of goats. The milk which these beasts supplied was tuberculosis free and thus specially recommended for patients suffering from consumption, the dreaded illness of the 19th century. It was also believed that those who came to drink the milk benefited from the clean clear air of the Ochil Hills and so often chose to stay for weeks at a time, finding accommodation in the many rooming or lodging houses which accommodated them in the village. While many residents rented rooms, unlike in Bridge of Allan, hotels were not established and so Blairlogie remained the small village which nowadays contributes so much to its charm.

Dedication

Dedicated to Jim Gauld, Chairman of the Strathallan Gathering and his wife Margaret.

Acknowledgements

My thanks to George and Rae McIntosh and Robin Kelsall for information about Blairlogie. Thanks also to Jim Gauld who provided the pictures on the inside back cover.

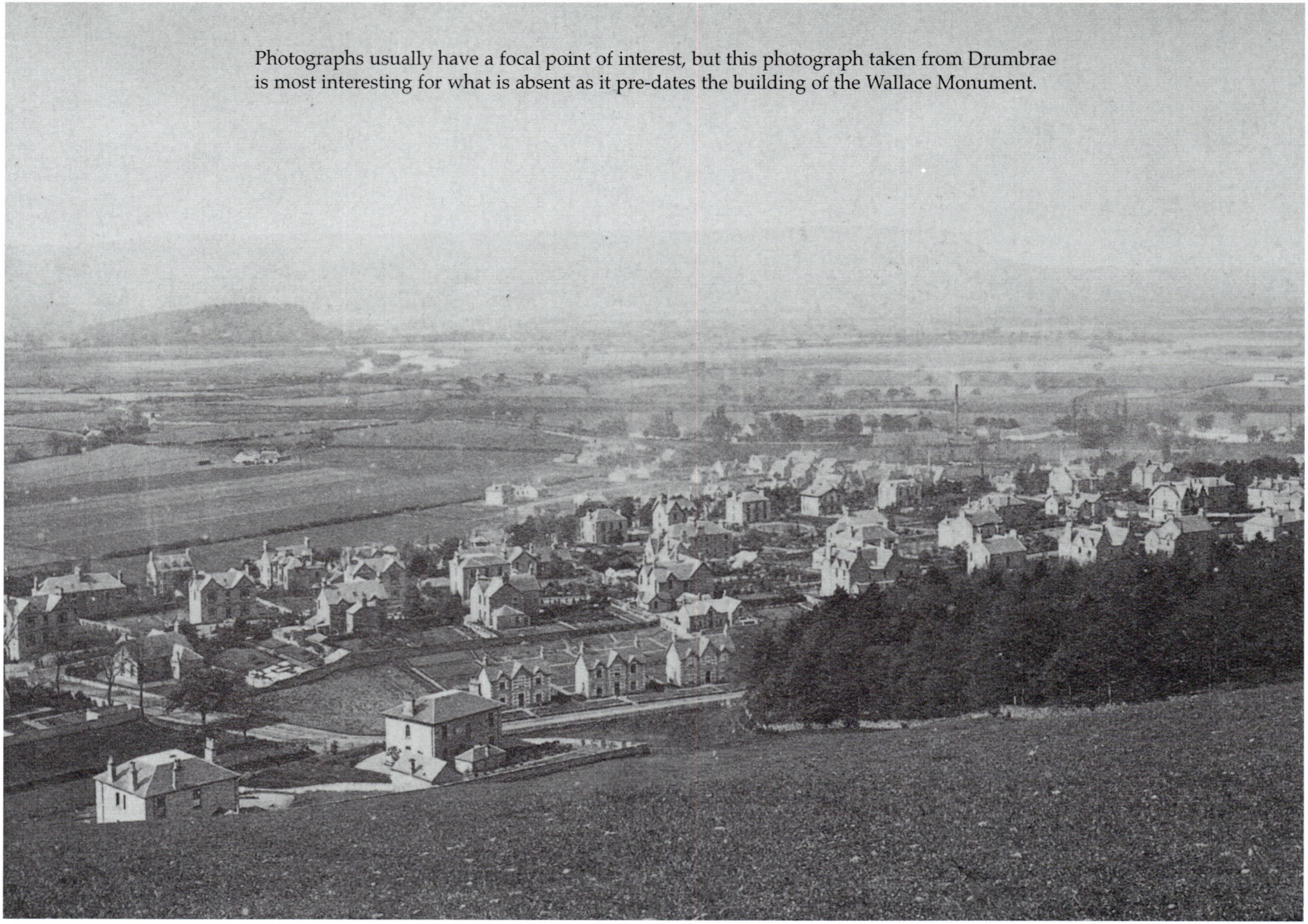

Photographs usually have a focal point of interest, but this photograph taken from Drumbrae is most interesting for what is absent as it pre-dates the building of the Wallace Monument.

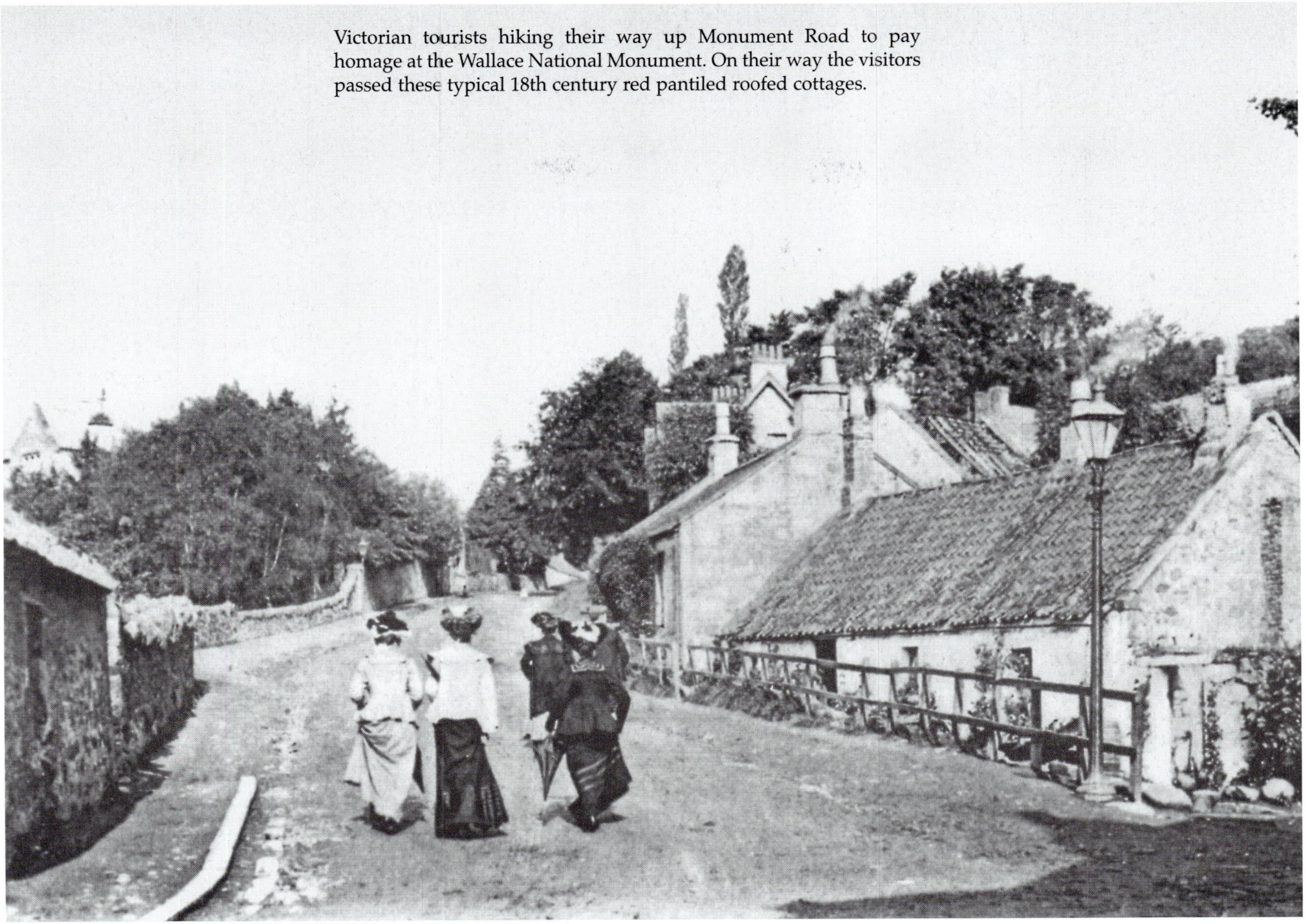

Victorian tourists hiking their way up Monument Road to pay homage at the Wallace National Monument. On their way the visitors passed these typical 18th century red pantiled roofed cottages.

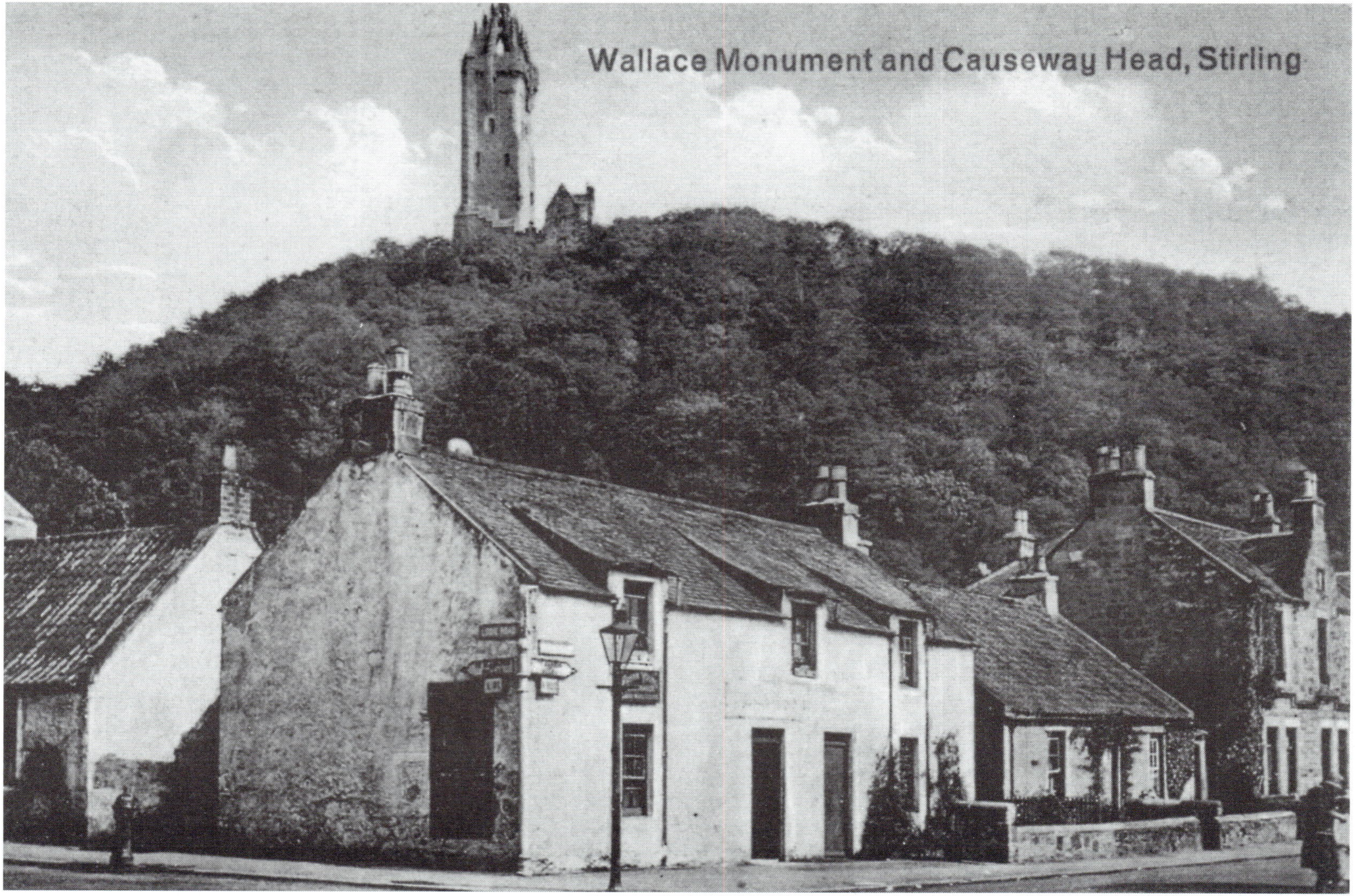

The Wallace National Monument also dominates this view of Causeway Head, where Corrieres popular Italian restaurant, ice cream parlour and fish and chip shop has since replaced the single storey cottage seen beyond the old two storey building on the corner of the road .

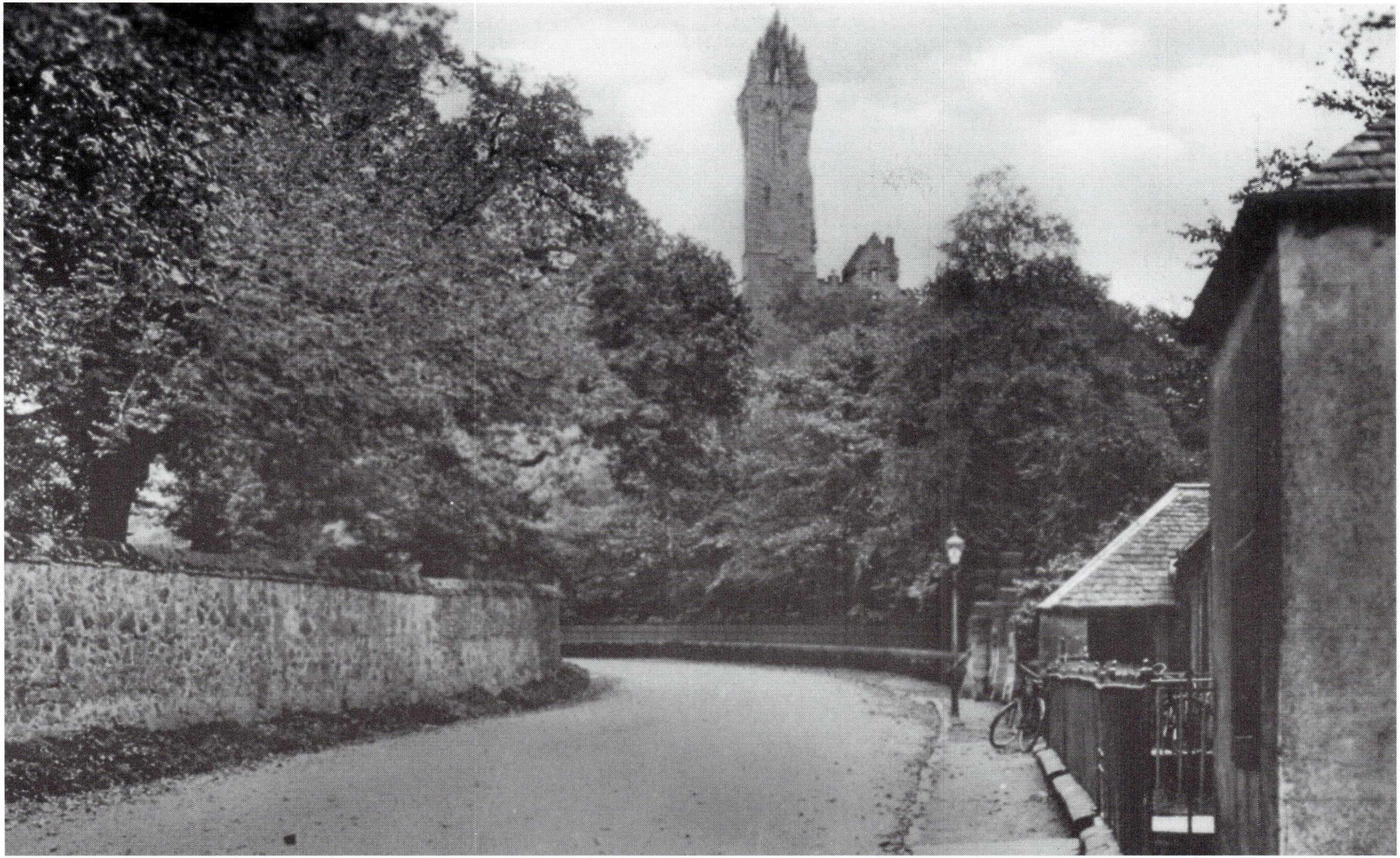

The Wallace National Monument stands four square dominating the scene in this view taken from Hillfoot Road. It was erected on Abbey Craig during the 1860s in time to commemorate the 600th anniversary of the celebrated Scottish hero's great victory over the English army at the Battle of Stirling Bridge in 1297. Built in Scottish Baronial style its features include a display about Wallace's famous massive seven foot long double bladed claymore sword, the Hall of Heroes and an exhibition detailing the construction of its impressive turreted tower. The tower is now accepted as a Scottish icon and a national landmark, but there was controversy over its design in Victorian times.

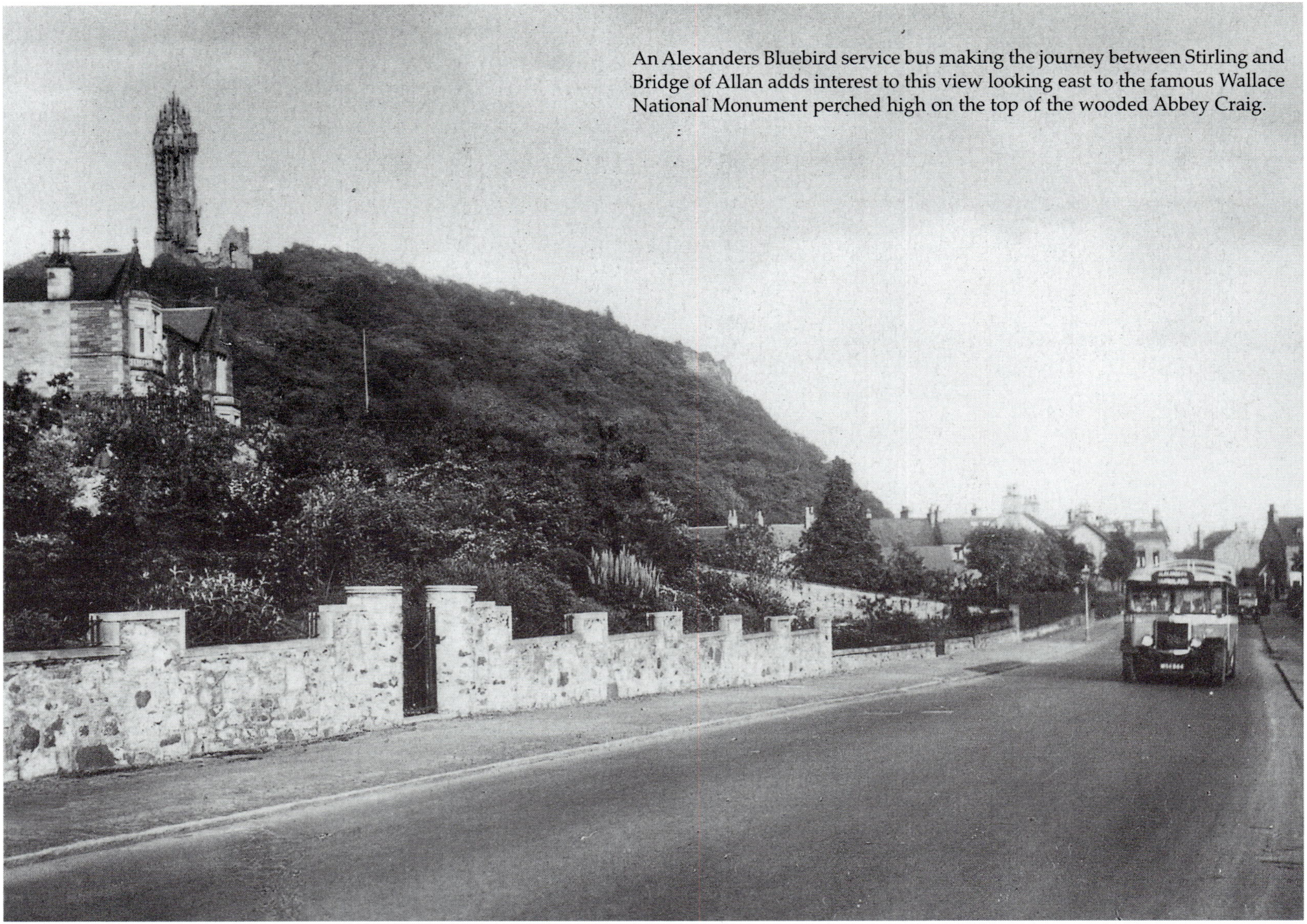

An Alexanders Bluebird service bus making the journey between Stirling and Bridge of Allan adds interest to this view looking east to the famous Wallace National Monument perched high on the top of the wooded Abbey Craig.

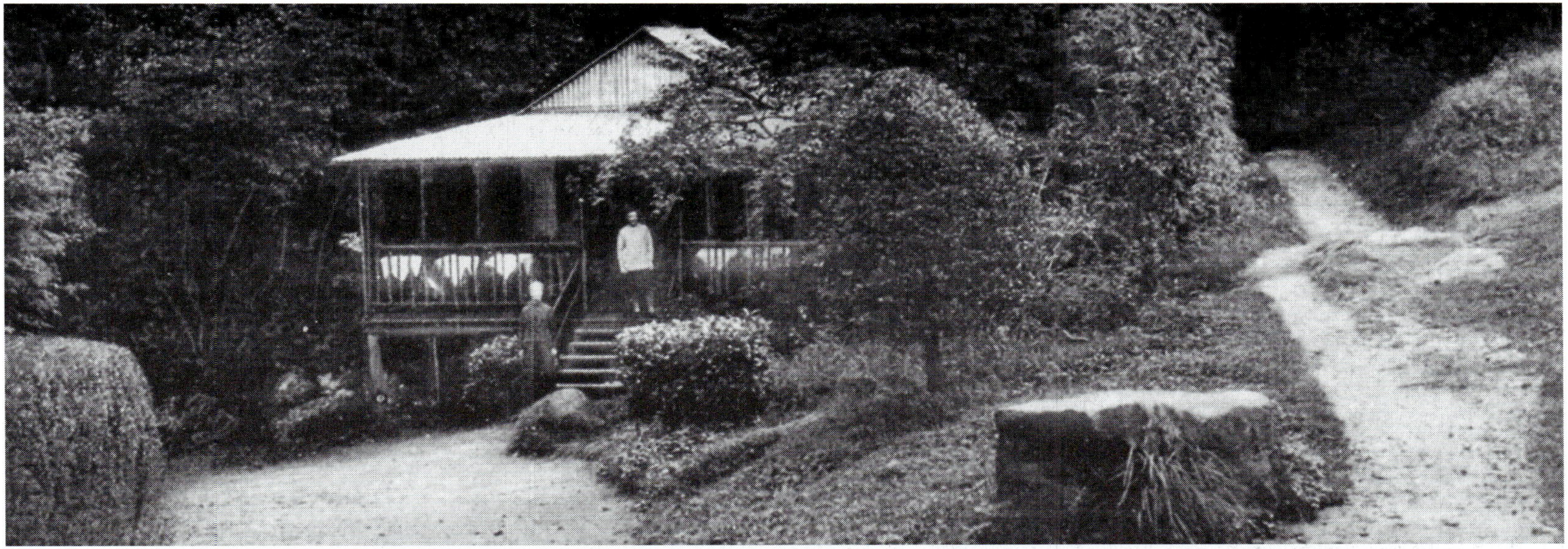

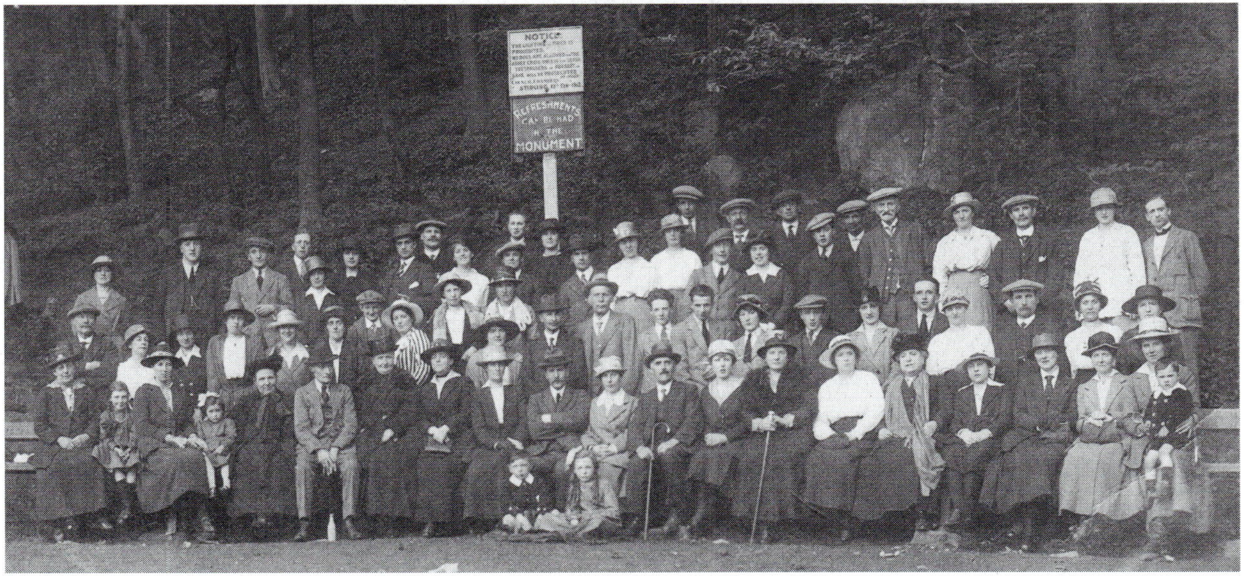

This Victorian wooden tea-room used to offer refreshments to the many visitors who toiled their way up the steep slopes to the summit of Abbey Craig to visit the Wallace National Monument. A feature of the grounds nowadays is a statue of William Wallace, which many visitors consider resembles Australian actor, Mel Gibson, who played the role of Wallace in the film Braveheart. The Abbey Craig used to be the source of stone for many of the milestones which measured distances along stage coach routes.

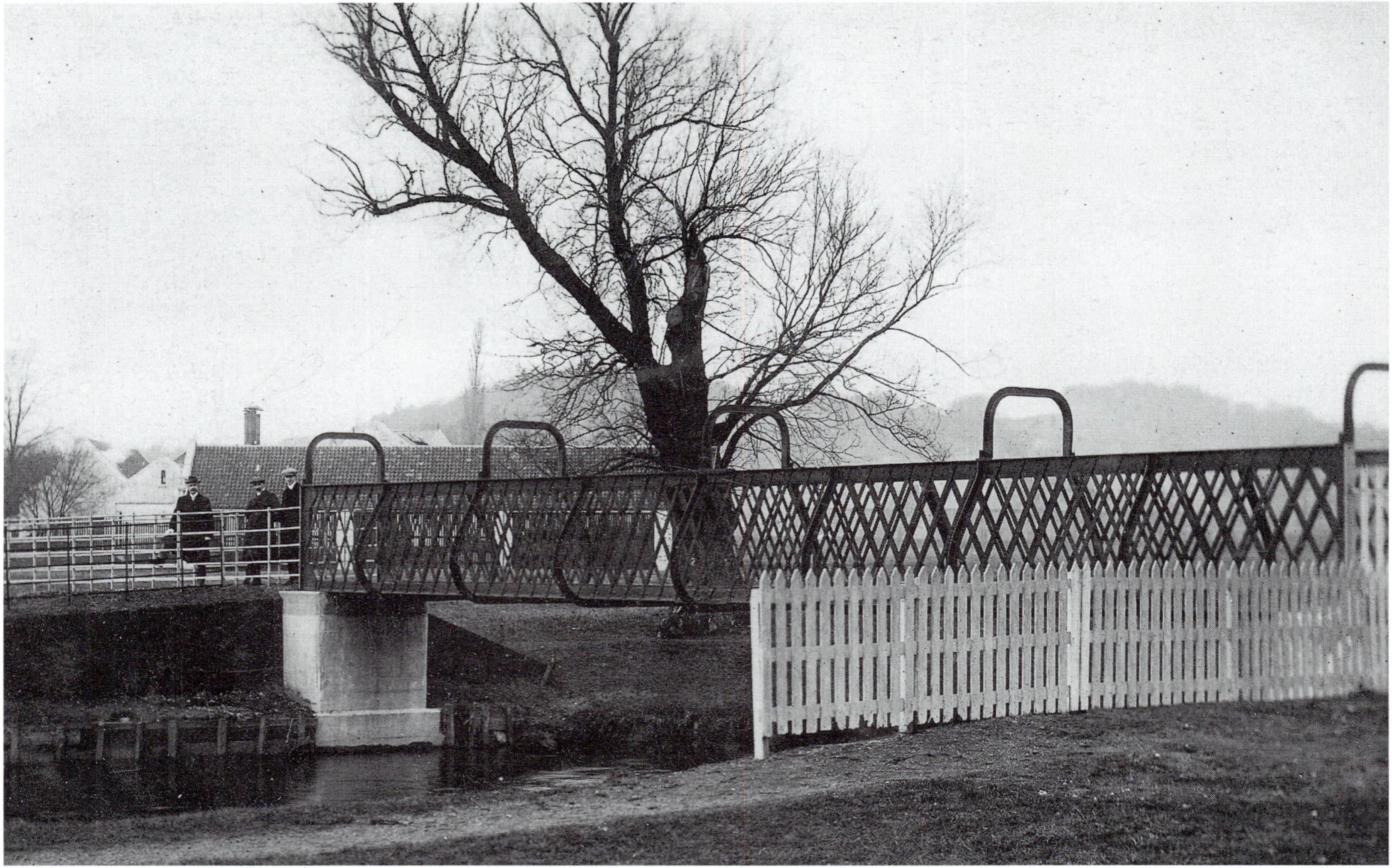

This iron bridge over the River Allan replaced two earlier wooden structures swept away by the floods which used to be an almost annual troublesome winter happening. The flood relief scheme instituted in the 1980s has done much to relieve the problem. The White Bridge, as it has always been known, was needed to enable workers to reach Pullars bleaching factory and also Keirfield Farm. However, as can bee seen from this old photograph it hasn't always been white. Currently Stirling Council has painted the bridge bright blue, but to Bridge of Allan residents it is still The White Bridge.

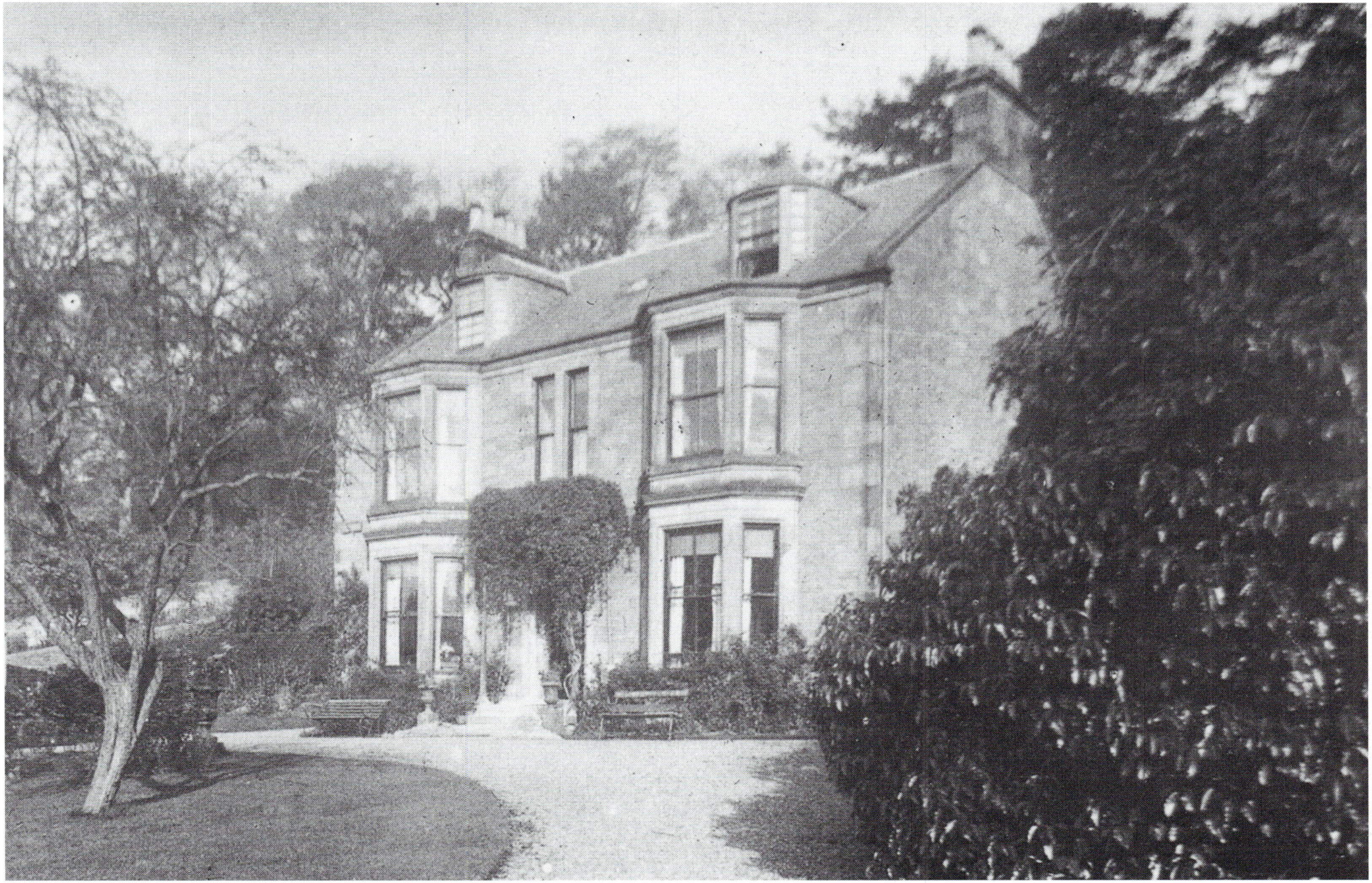

This attractive Victorian villa was one of many built along Henderson Street. Its three storied facade with bay windows on either side made it one of the most imposing of the villas and it is now even more spacious as a modern stone fronted extension has been added to the right. Eagleton is now an annexe of the Royal Hotel, with bedrooms and conferences facilities.

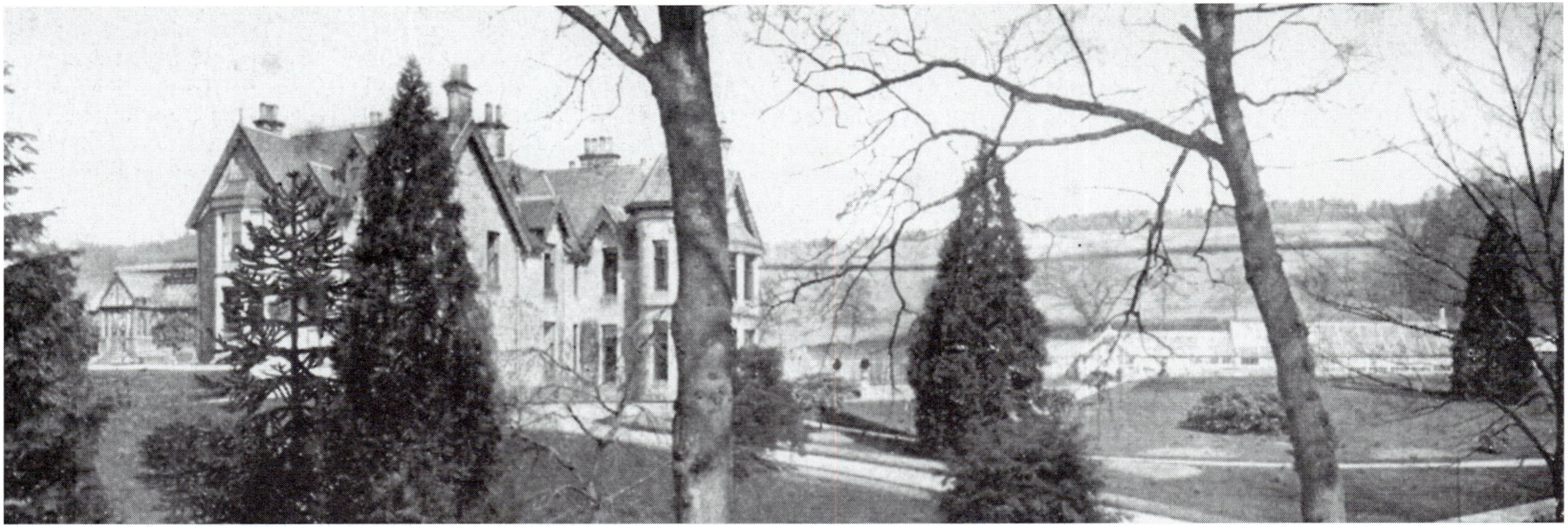

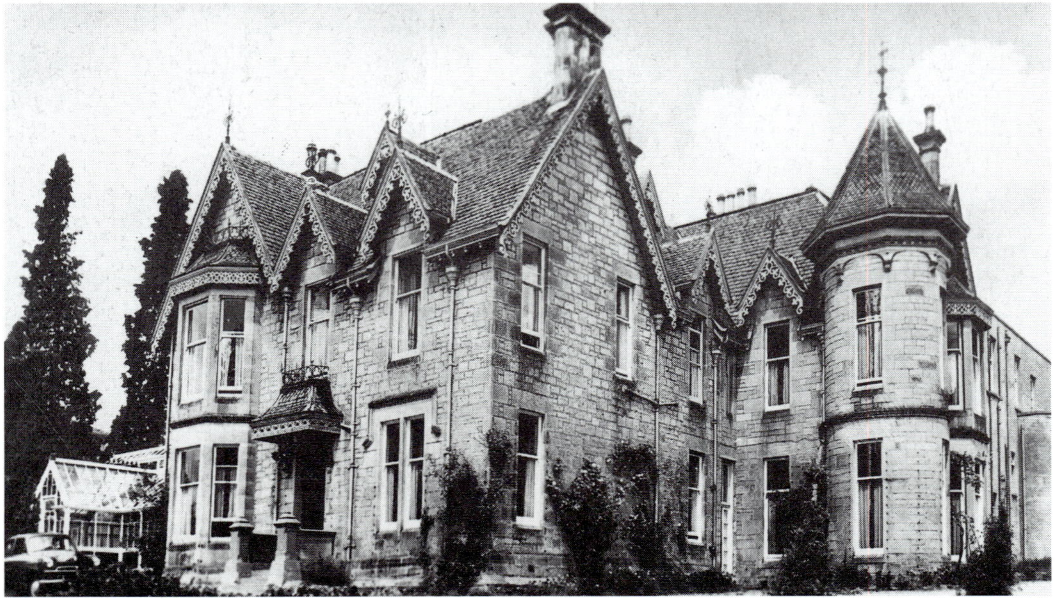

The Alangrange Hotel is seen here on two postcard views. Notice the stylish overhanging eaves above the three first floor front windows, the two bay windows on both ground and first floor and the canopied entrance porch above the front door. The tower on the right adds a touch of Scottish Baronial to the appearance also. During the early years of the university's existence the singularly spelt Alangrange Hotel was converted into the original Student Union building. The building's interior has since been redesigned to form spacious high ceilinged apartments.

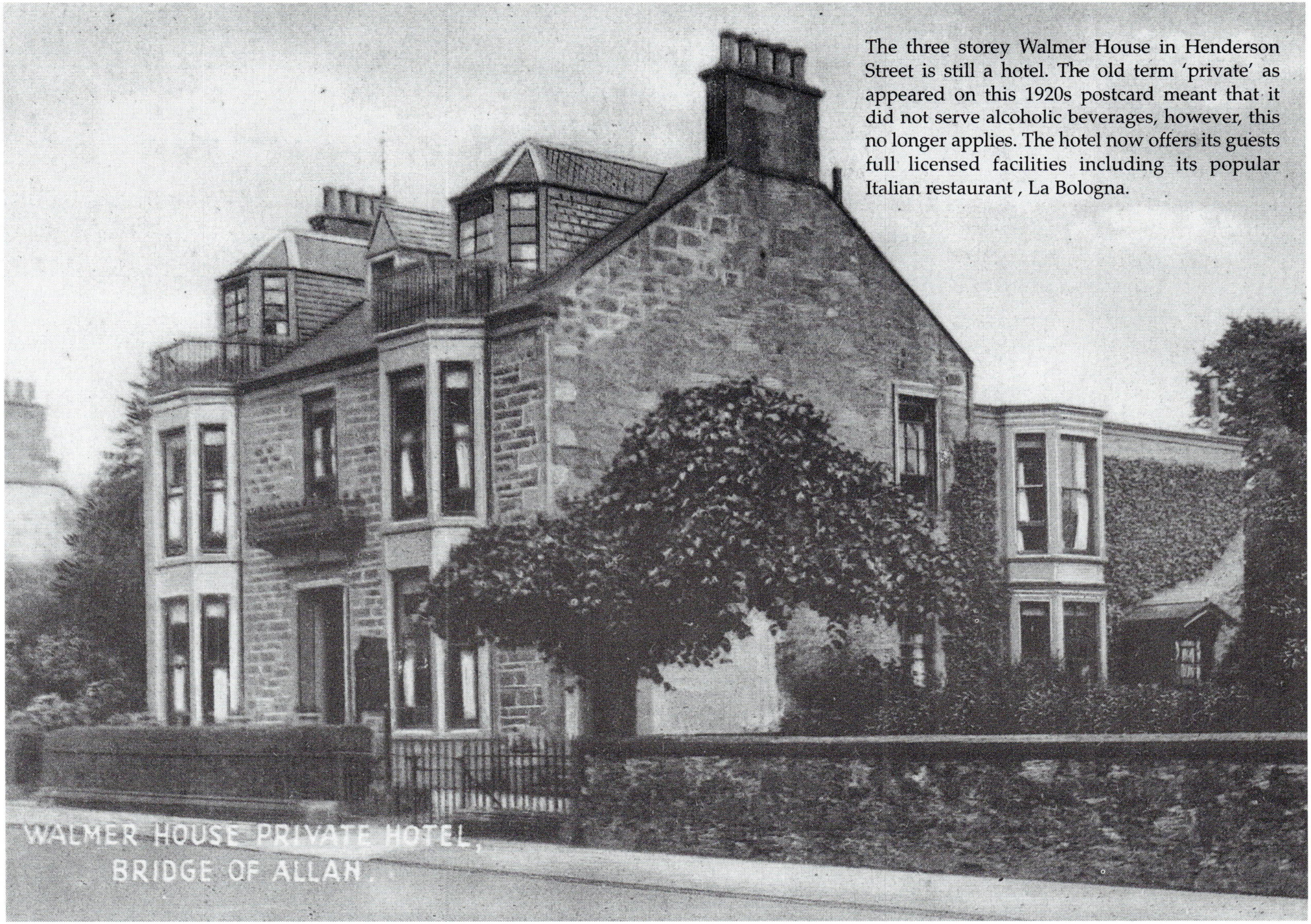

The three storey Walmer House in Henderson Street is still a hotel. The old term 'private' as appeared on this 1920s postcard meant that it did not serve alcoholic beverages, however, this no longer applies. The hotel now offers its guests full licensed facilities including its popular Italian restaurant , La Bologna.

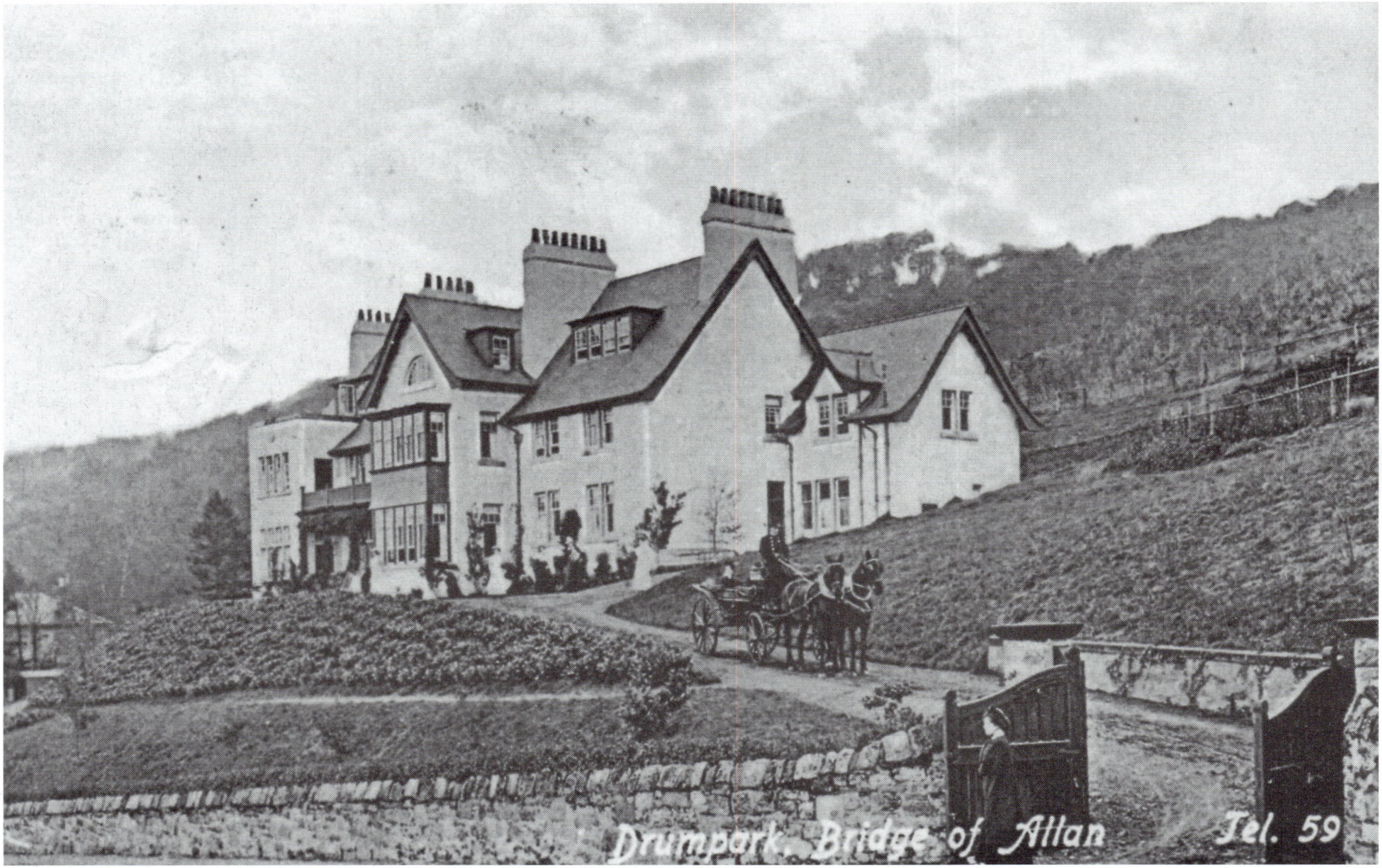

A horse-drawn carriage with its smartly liveried coachman clip clops down the drive from Drumpark. This large villa in Claremont Road was originally known as Salen House and was the premises of Ramsey's Sanatorium. Many patients suffering from tuberculosis came here for the fresh hill air which the town offered in the decades before the 1940s and the discovery of streptomycin and other effective drugs. Part of the treatment offered by Ramsey's sanatorium was for these patients to lie in beds outdoors on the verandas which were south facing so as to attract maximum sunshine.

Ramsay's Studio still stands in Union Street and survives having been converted to offices and later houses. The mock-Tudor building with its black and white magpie woodwork and overhanging eaves was erected in 1888 as a photographic studio and art gallery by Colin Ramsay, who owned another studio in Glasgow. The Studio can be seen on the left of the upper picture of Union street taken in 1905. The successful business was subsequently run for many years by Mr. Ramsay's son, before being acquired in 1921 by photographer George Hughes.

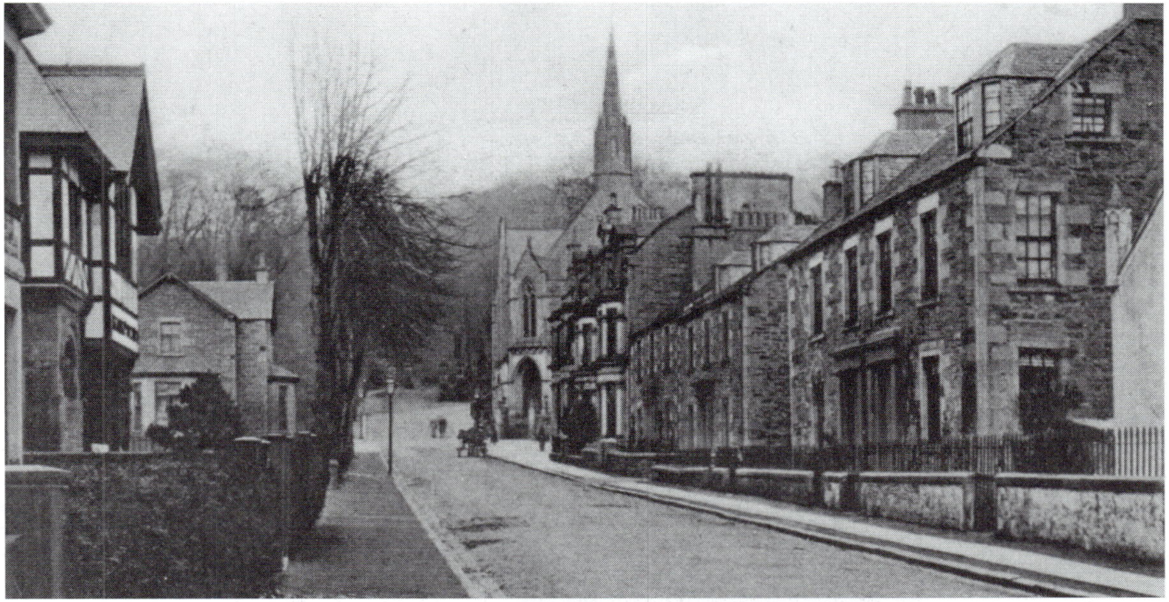

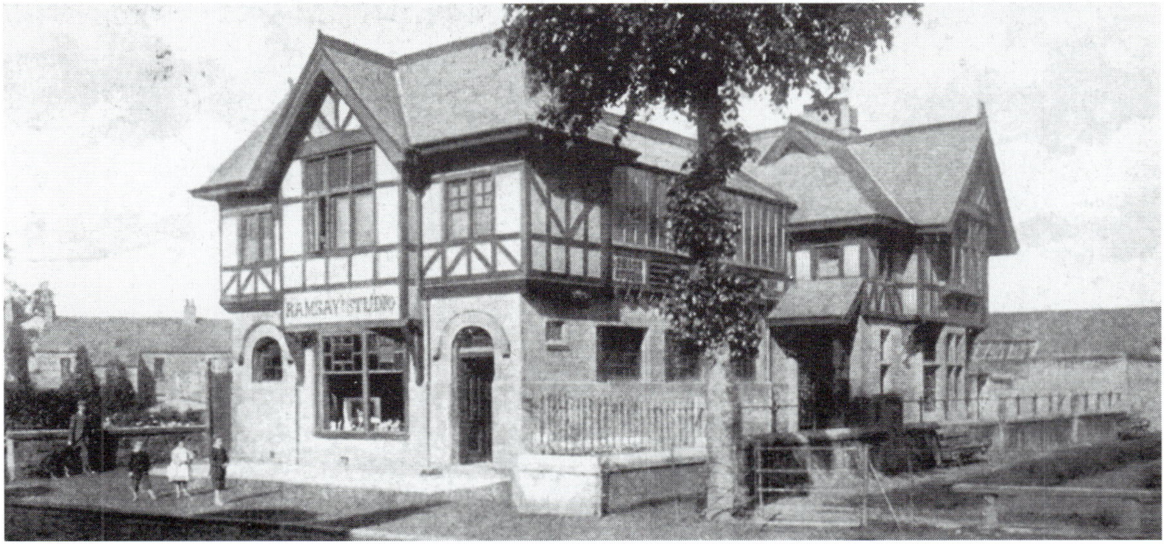

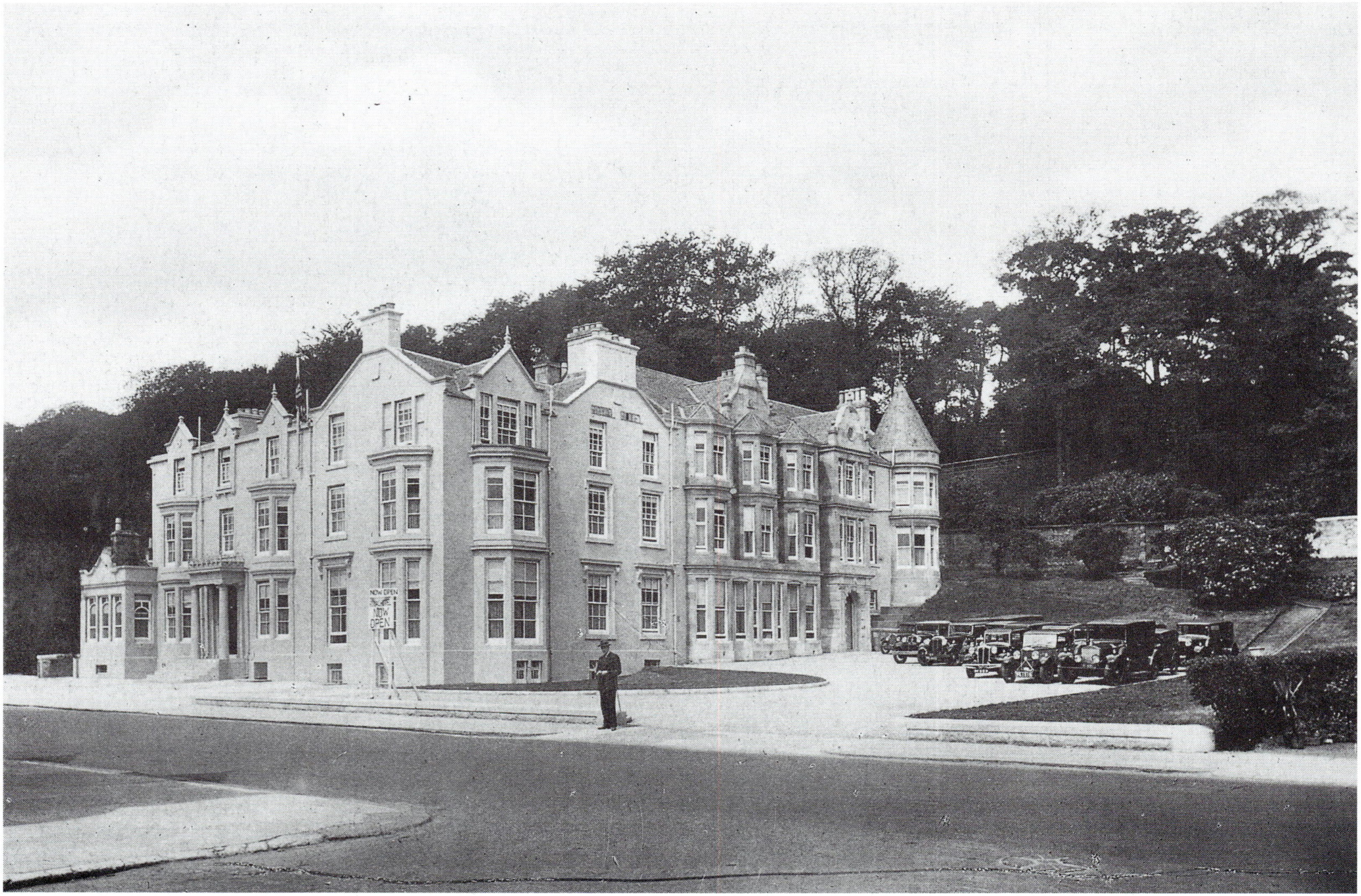

The Royal Hotel was founded by Mr. Philp in 1842, following the success of his original smaller Philps Hotel in the town. Visitors during Queen Victoria's reign included Charles Dickens and Robert Louis Stevenson.

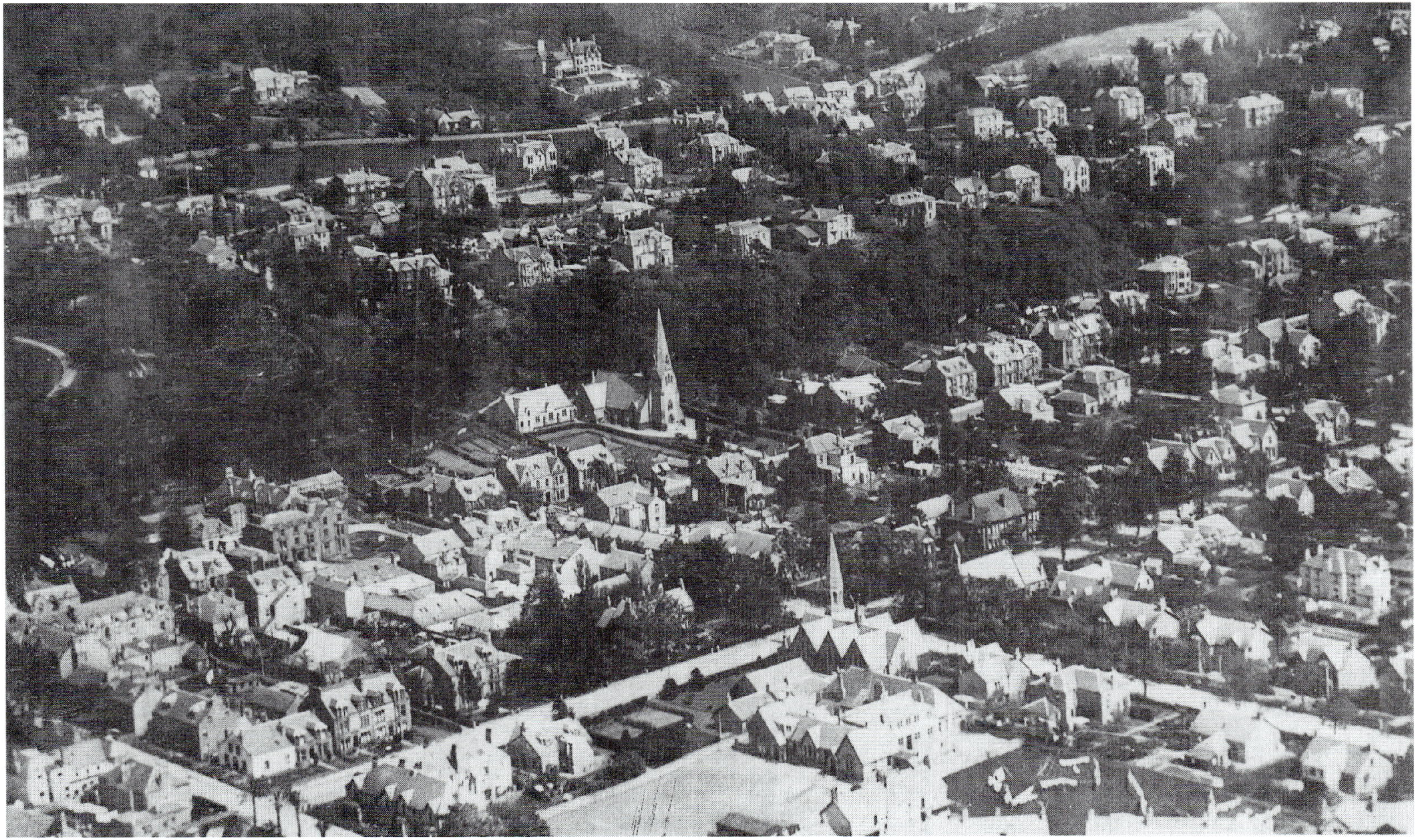

Taken from the south west this aerial photograph provides an excellent panoramic view of the prosperous spa town as it was in the 1930s. In the foreground is the former Bridge of Allan Primary School and its playground, now the Community Centre. Directly behind the old school rises the steeple of Holy Trinity Parish Church at the junction of Keir Street and Fountain Road. On the opposite corner of Fountain Road to Trinity can be made out the premises of St. Saviours Scottish Episcopal Church. In the centre of the picture is Chalmers Church, on the north side of Henderson Street, which runs diagonally across the picture, the grounds and buildings of the former Hydro, are to the left of the spire, and the town's many substantially built Victorian villas on the wooded hilside behind it.

Fountain Road takes its name from the impressive cast iron Fountain of Ninevah installed by Major Henderson. Important archaeological discoveries in Assyria in Turkey in the 1840s coincided with his development of the planned village of Bridge of Allan.

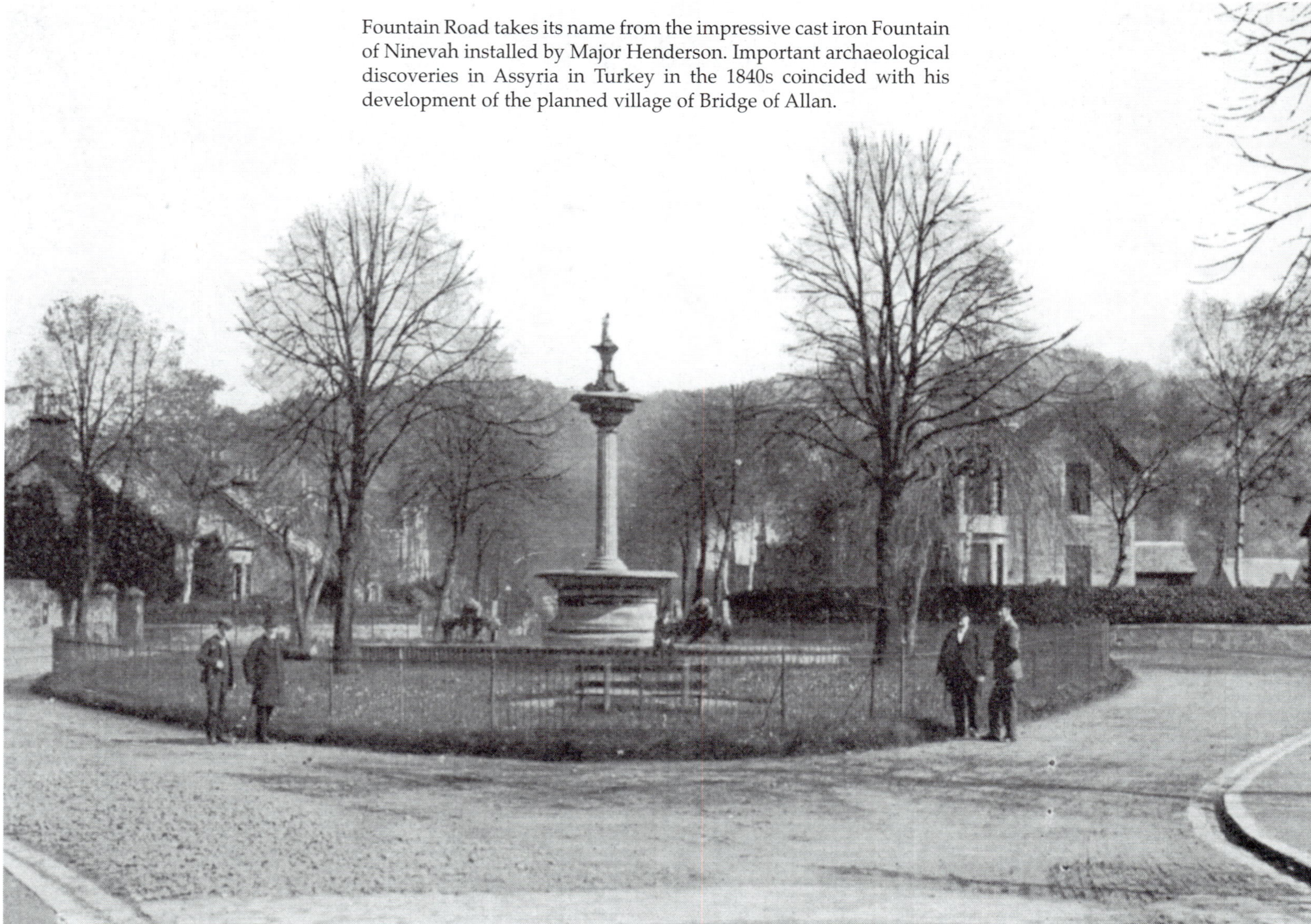

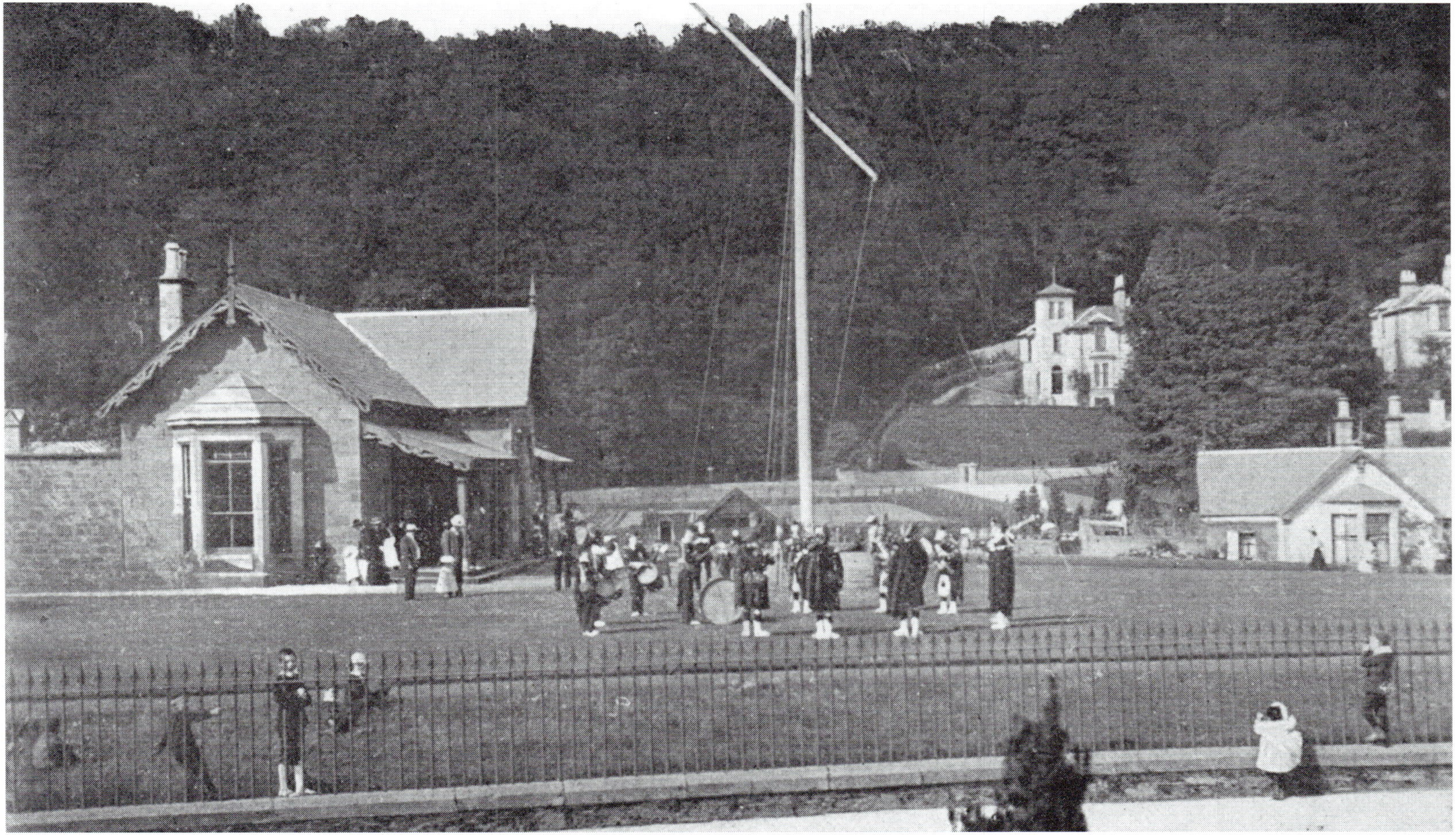

This circa 1905 view shows a local pipe band playing on a summer evening on the lawn in front of what is described as the Wells House in the grounds of the Hydro. More usually referred to as the Spa House, this building now houses the popular Chambo Restaurant. On the wooded hillside can be seen two villas, Woodlee and Ardfardash, with the club house of the Airthrey Spa Bowling Club glimpsed (behind the flag pole). Nowadays the Strathallan Gathering, the town's most popular summer event and held on the first Sunday in August, often attracts more than seventy pipe bands and their mass parade is always the climax of the town's Highland Games. This is the final event before the World Pipe Band Championships held on the following Saturday , hence the large numbers of bands which attend. Known as the Last Blaw, the games at Bridge of Allan provides the pipers and drummers with an ideal setting to practise and perfect their paling before participating in the championships.

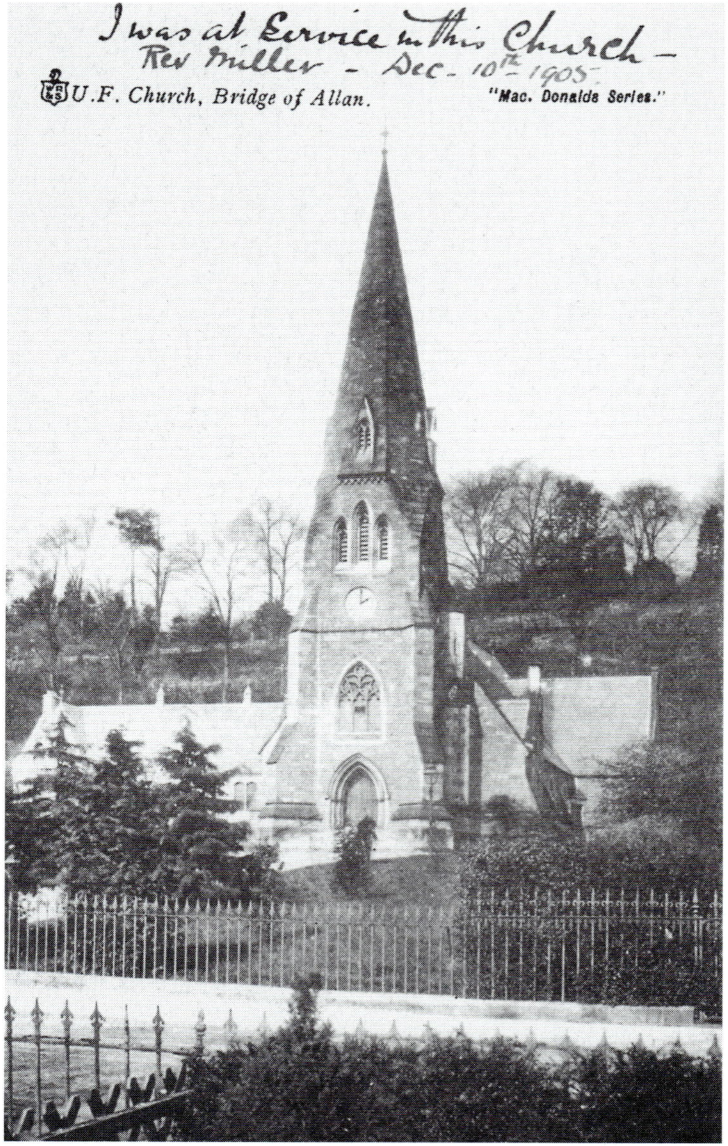

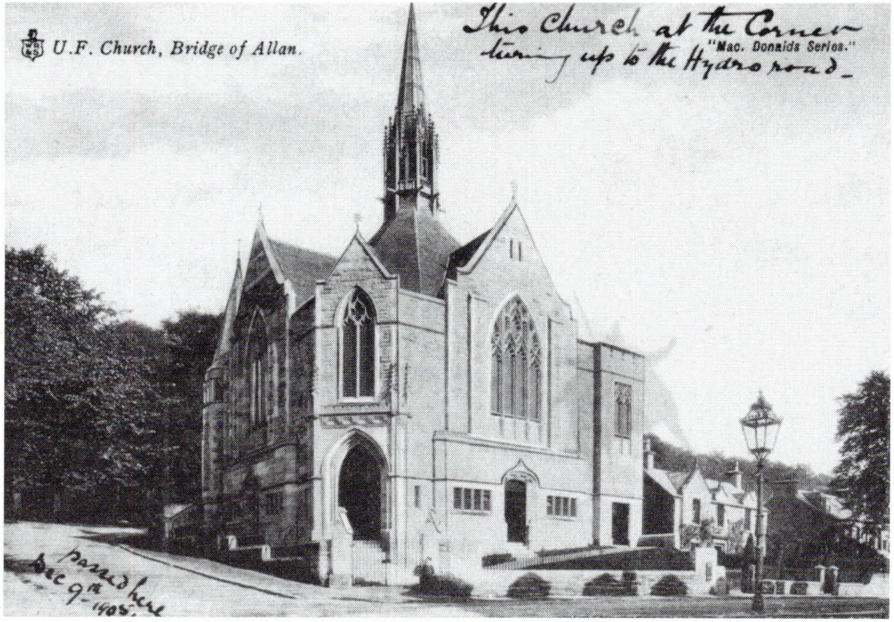

Bridge of Allan was originally served by two parish churches, both outside the boundaries of the village. To the east was Logie Kirk and to the west Lecropt. It was not until after the Disruption of the Church of Scotland in 1843, caused by a dispute over whether local lairds or members of the congregations had the right to choose ministers, that the creation of the Free Kirk led to the construction of new churches such as the former Chalmers Church (*left*) shown here.

The United Presbyterian Church (*above*: wrongly captioned as the United Free Church) oversaw the scene in the centre of Bridge of Allan until 1948, when it had to be demolished due to the foundations being damaged by underground springs pouring down the hillside. The church stood at the junction of Henderson Street and the steep road leading up to the Allan Water Hotel and was often referred to as "The Church on the Corner".

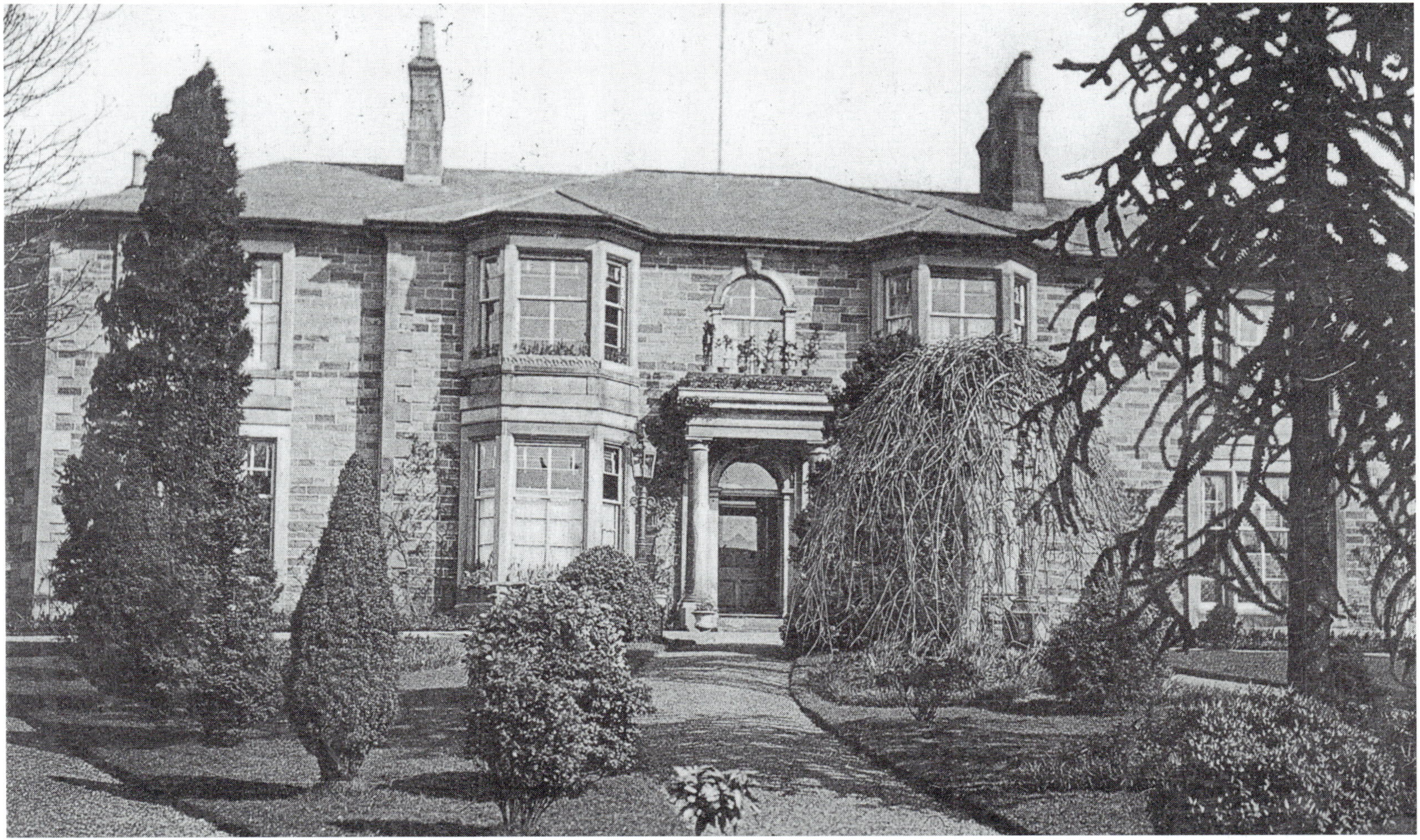

Stanley House in Henderson Street was a boarding school for boys. Clad in their bright scarlet blazers and grey flannel shorts with red stockings, the boys were a familiar sight in town until the school went bankrupt in 1939. In 1941 its premises were re-opened temporarily to provide accommodation for boys and girls hurriedly evacuated from Clydebank after the 1941 blitz of Clydeside by the Luftwaffe. After the war Stanley House was converted into private apartments as was its dormitory annexe in Prospect House, the former Prospect Villa Lodging House on the opposite side of the street. Next door, Birnock was the scene of a notorious murder when on the night of the Strathallan Gathering in August 1921 an intruder killed the elderly woman resident and assaulted her companion with a beer bottle. The murderer escaped and was never caught.

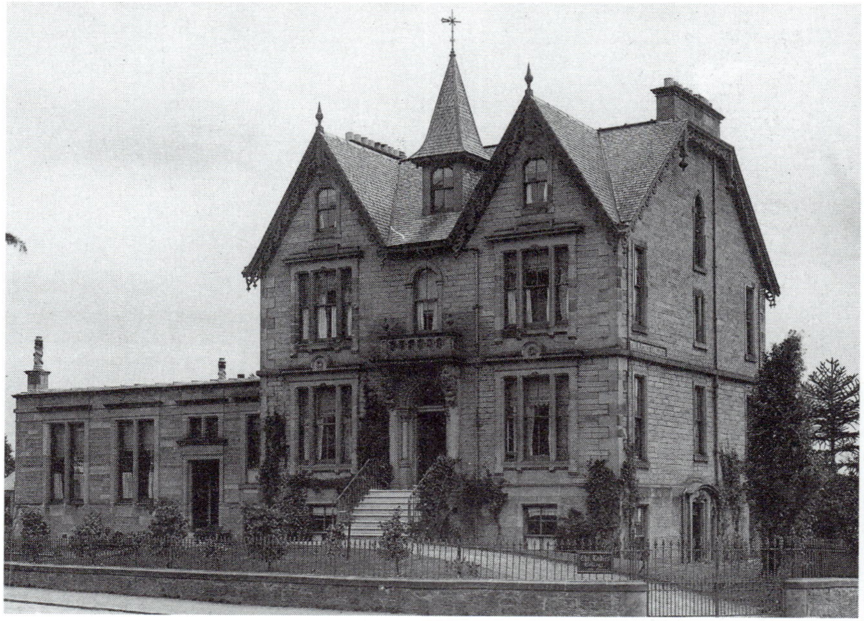

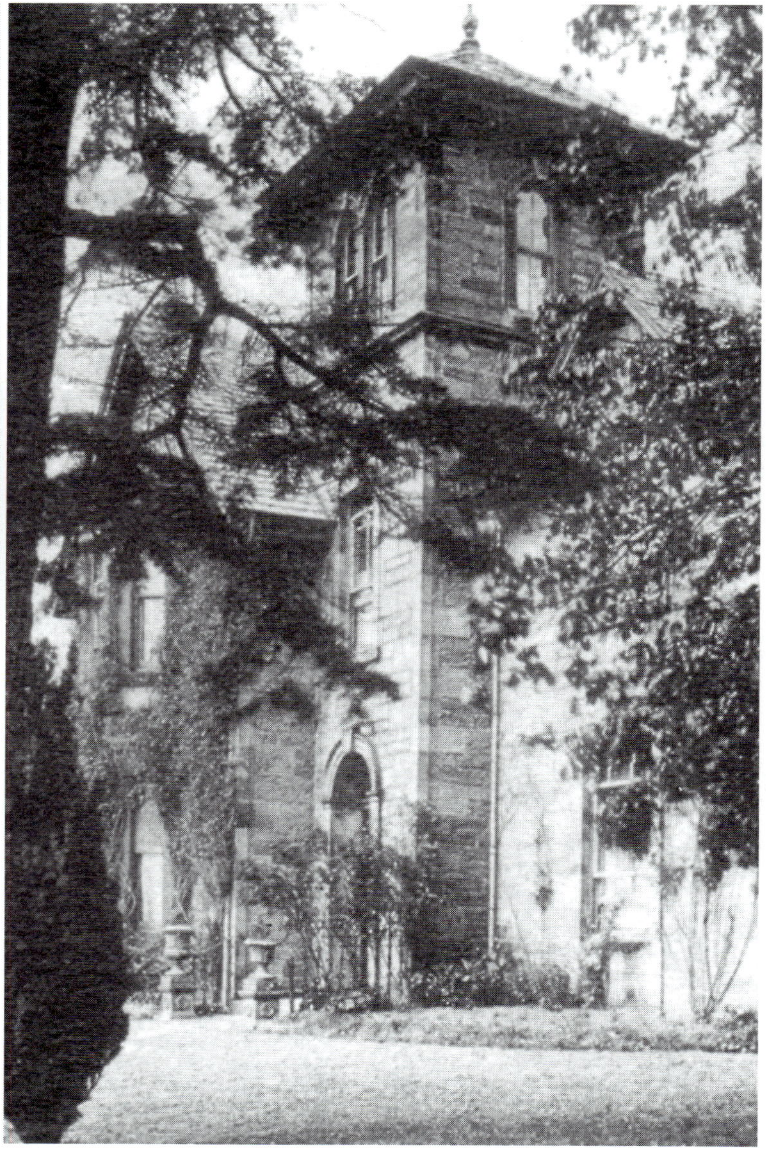

The Ladies College pictured above was also known as St. Helens School. This independent private school was so successful that a single storey extension was added as seen on the left. The Monkey Puzzle tree on the right was often set as a subject for the girls to sketch in their art classes.

Later other neighbouring villas were acquired to accommodate the increase in the number of girls who enrolled. The Junior House annex pictured right was one of these.

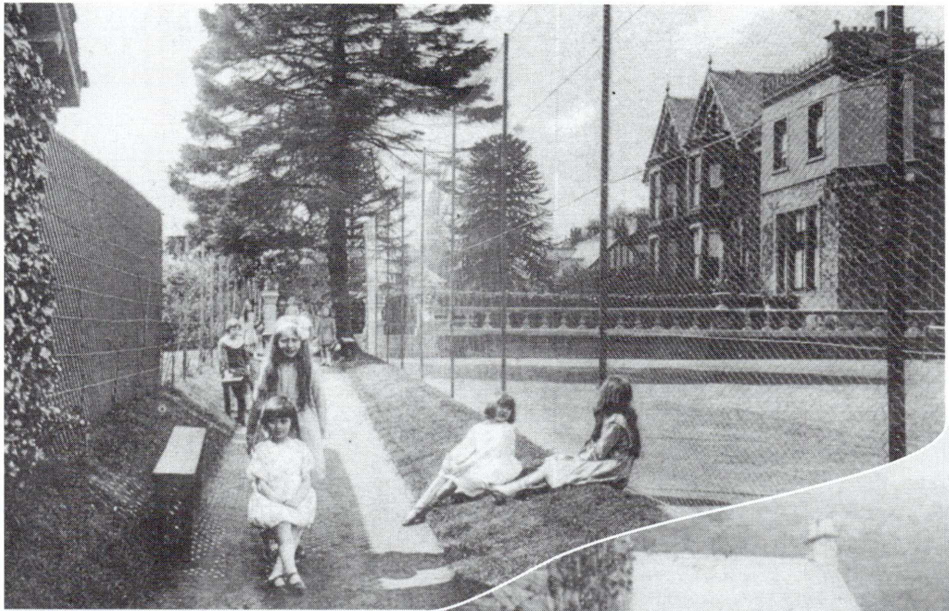

Just over the hedge of the gardens (below) was the schools sports field (left) on which the girls practised hockey and lacrosse. Tennis was also played in summer and netball during the winter months. Private education still flourishes in Bridge of Allan with Beaconhurst School in Kenilworth road offering an excellent education for pupils aged from nursery to sixth form.

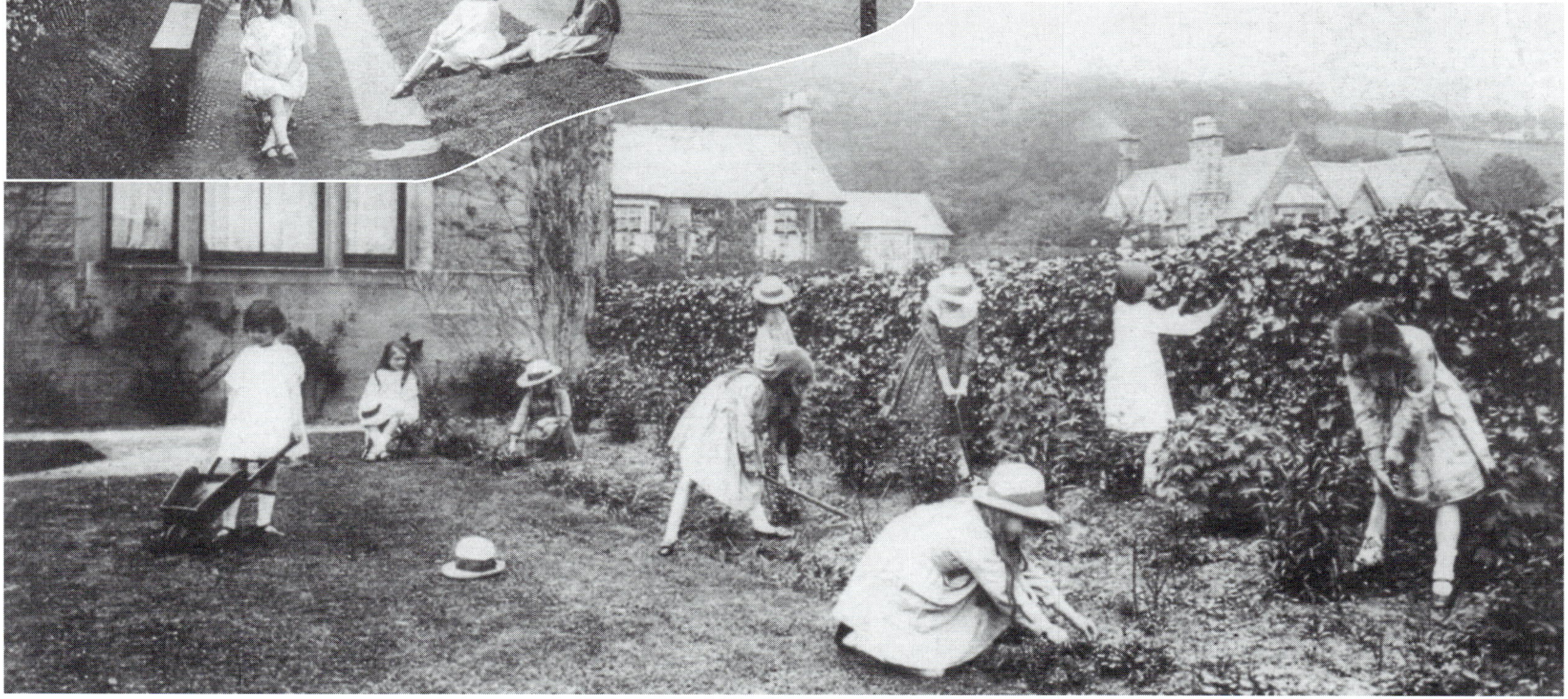

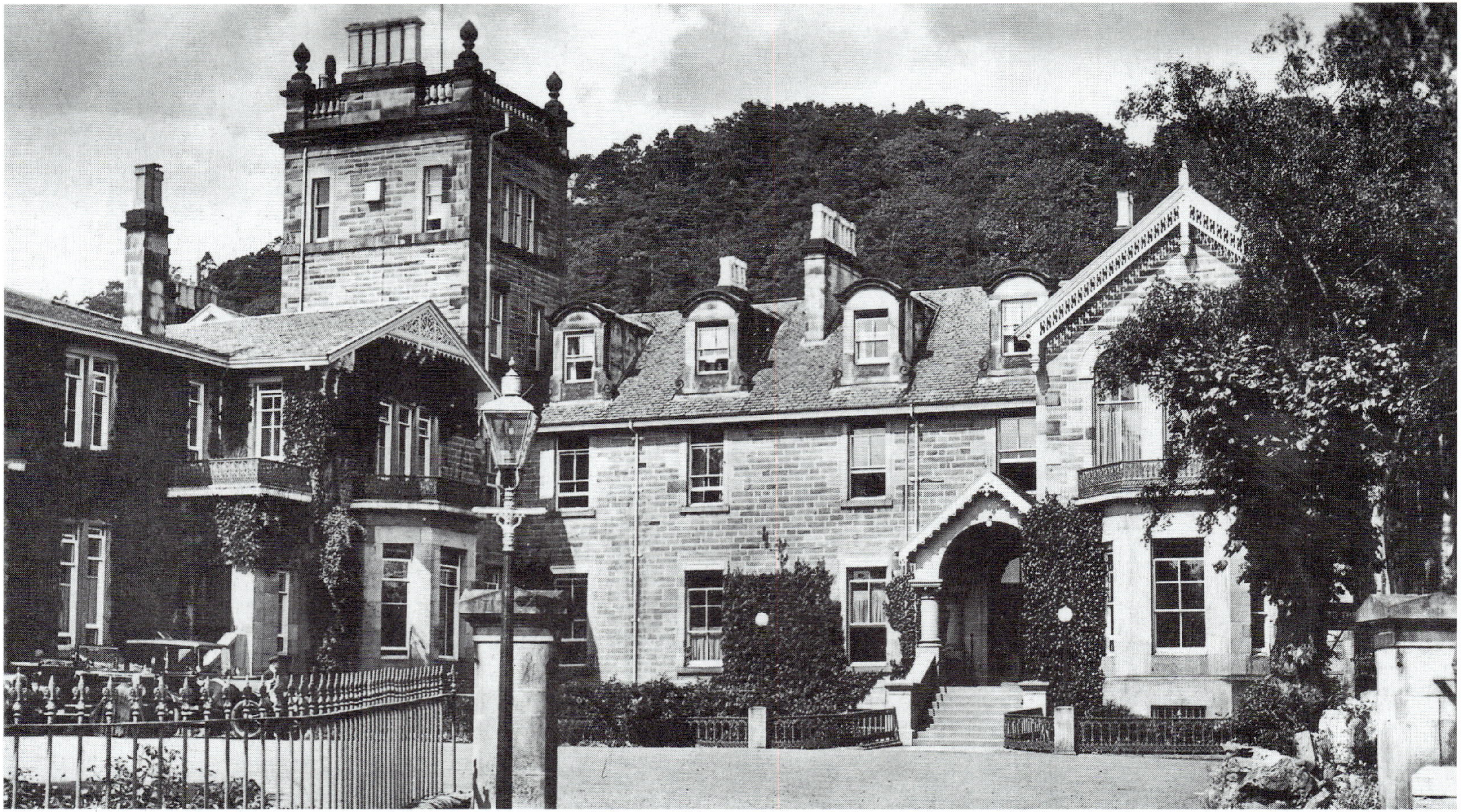

Opened in 1864, The Allan Water Hotel was originally known as the Ochil Hills Hyrdopathic Hotel. The bath house boasted a flow of 1,000 gallons a day of the health-giving water claimed to be beneficial for sufferers of health problems ranging from rheumatism to gout and from skin complaints to feeling bilious. At the height of its popularity the spa was visited by up to 500 people a day. During the Second World War the hotel was also requisitioned by the military authority as quarters for army officers. In 1946 the hotel was acquired by the Scottish Co-operative Wholesale Society, but it failed to flourish and was later converted into private apartments. Guests are, however, still welcome at the upmarket Chambo restaurant, whose spacious premises are housed in the original Spa House and in the attractive curved conservatory sun parlour which was a later Edwardian addition. The Spa House dates from 1861 and above the main entrance is a coat of arms depicting a bee surmounted by a crown. On the north side of the restaurant car park, the pumping house for the spa still also stands and a campaign is underway to secure its restoration.

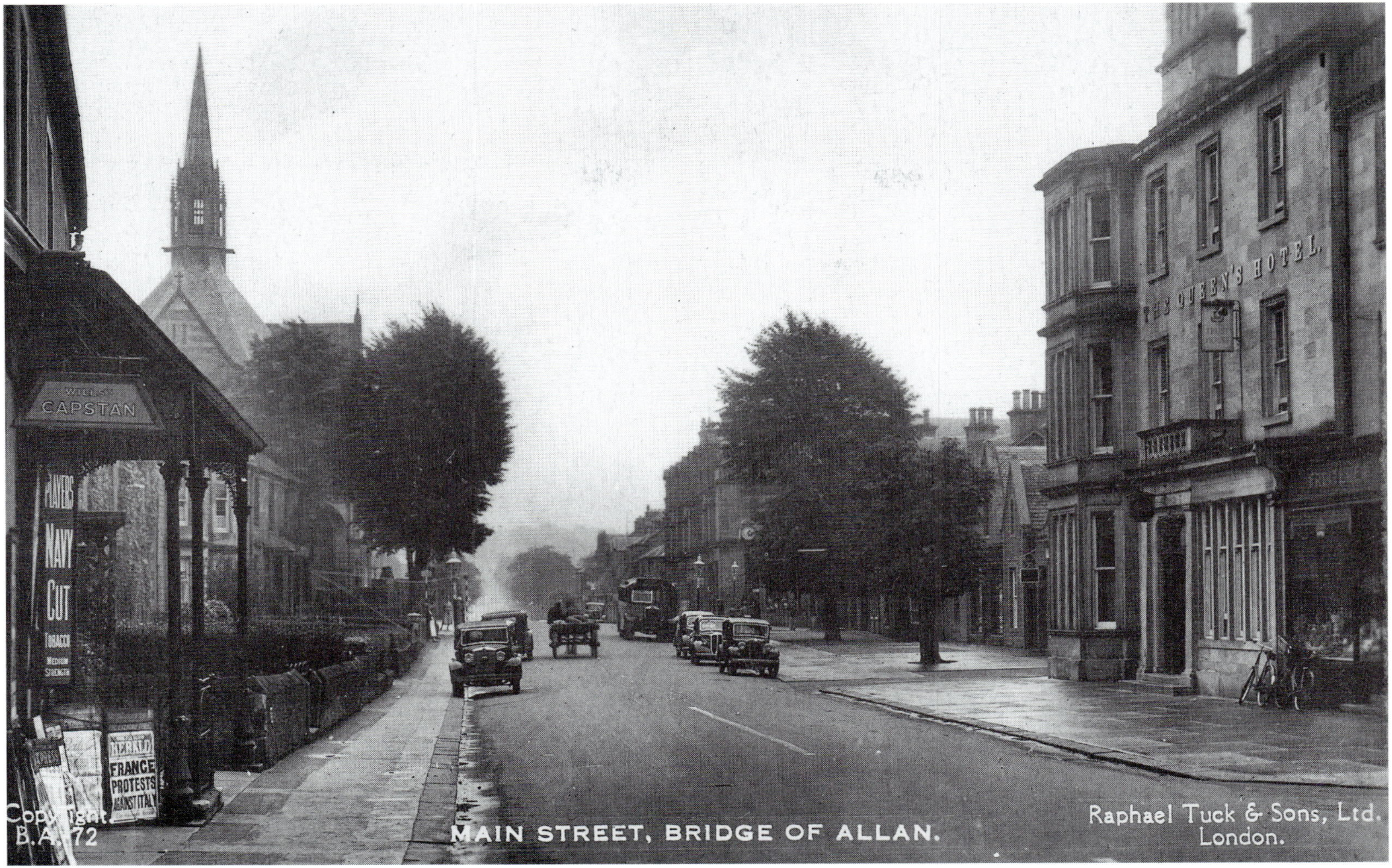

This view looks east along the length of Henderson Street, described here simply as Main Street and dates from the 1930s. The attractive premises on the left were demolished to make way for modern shops. Beyond them in the picture is the spire of the United Presbyterian Church, another landmark before it too was demolished.

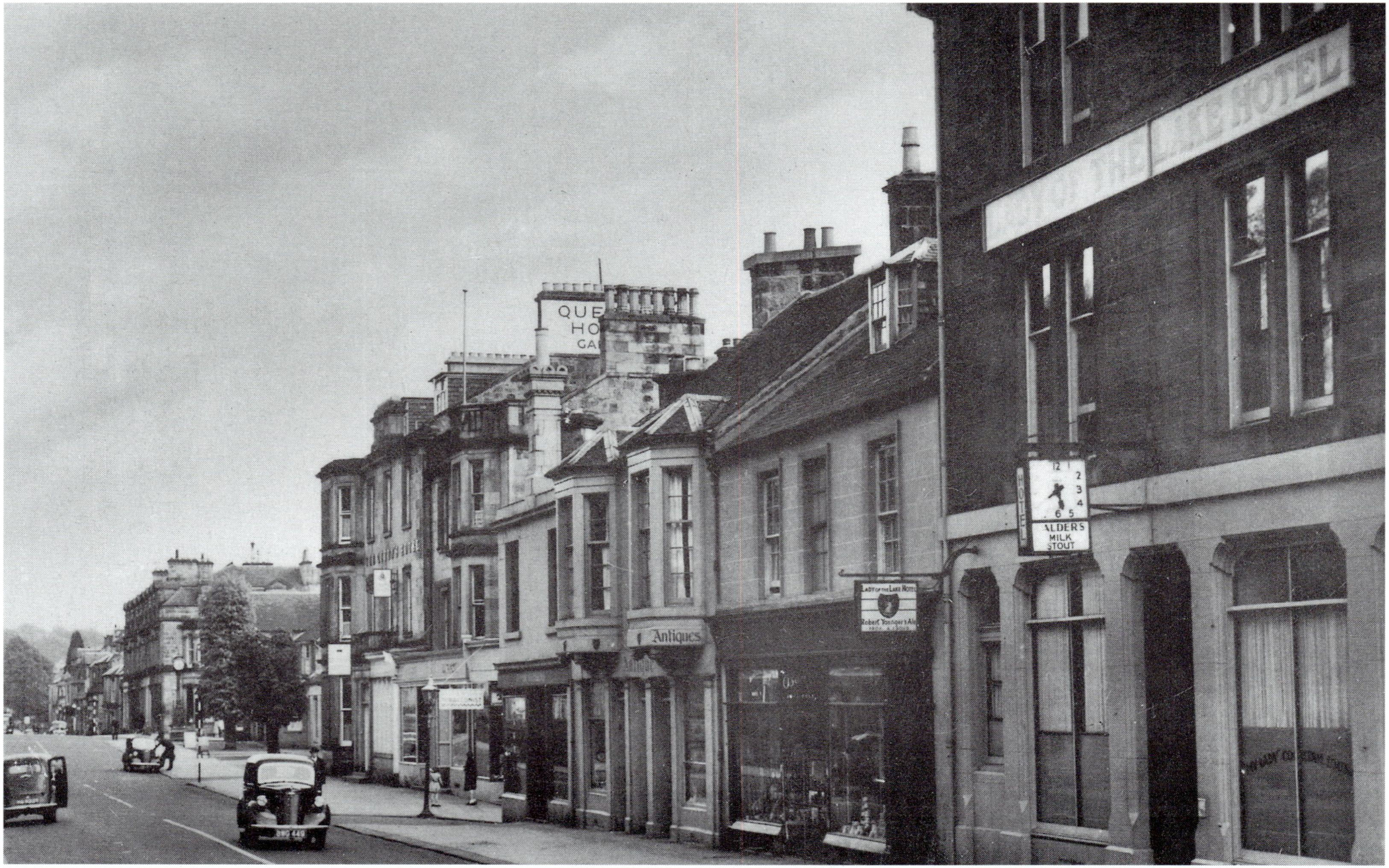

This view of the south side of the east end of Henderson Street shows two Bridge of Allan Hotels, the well known Queens and the smaller and now long forgotten Lady of the Lake, which took its name from Sir Walter Scott's famous ballad poem set in the Trossachs around Loch Katrine. The premises occupied by the latter have also over the years been home to W. Henderson's boot and shoe shop and more recently Bridge of Allan Books. It has now been converted into a hairdressing salon.

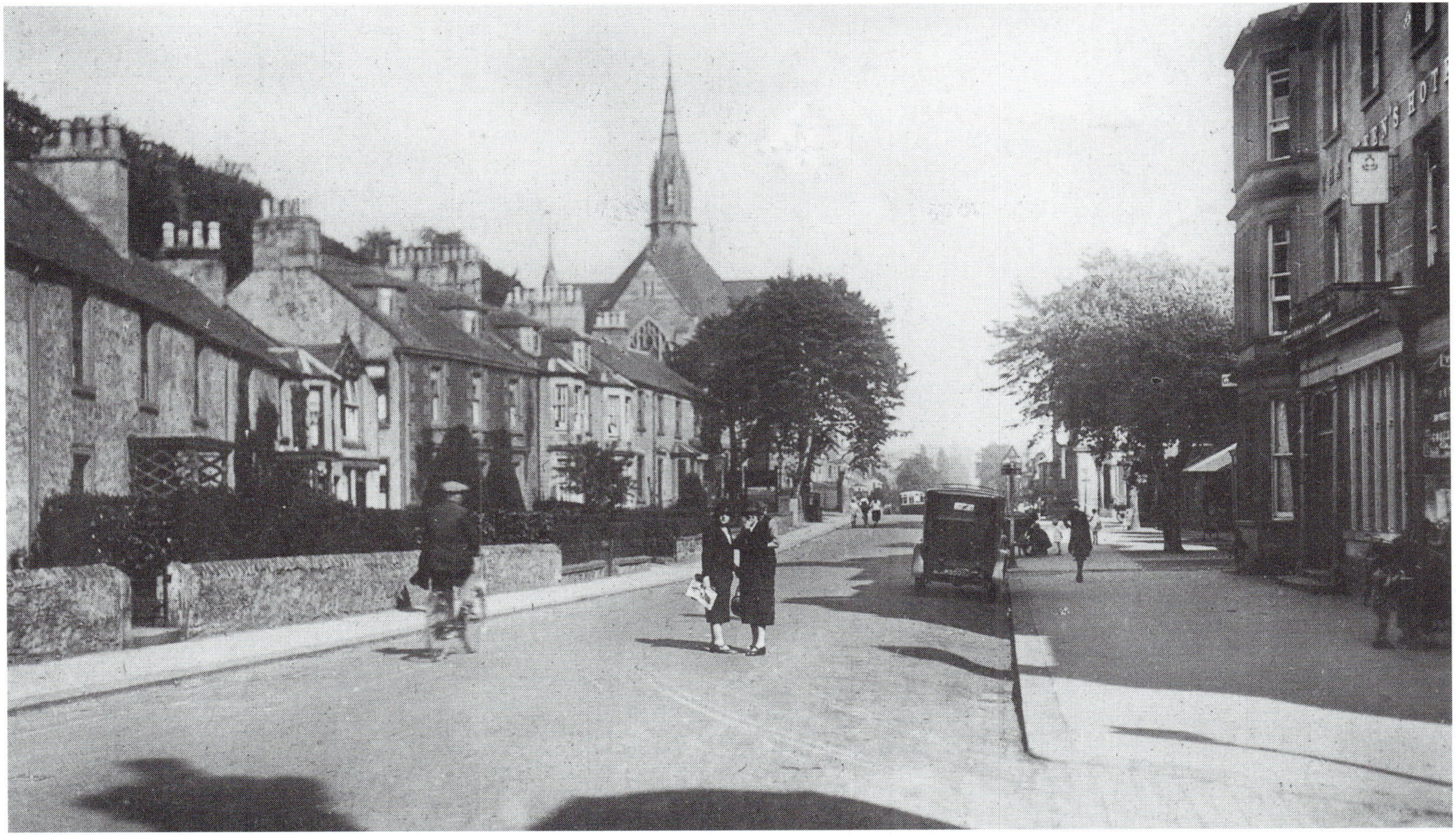

The properties on the left in this view looking east along Henderson Street have long been demolished. In Victorian times the post office stood on the south side of Henderson Street. It gained notoriety because it was there that Emile L'Anglelier, a young visitor from the Channel Islands, came to collect a post restante letter sent to him by his lover Madeleine Smith, who stayed with her family in Bridge of Allan for ten days in March 1857 at Prospect Villa on the south side of Henderson Street. The letter summoned him to her home in Glasgow, where it was later alleged that she had murdered him by poisoning his bedtime cocoa with arsenic. At her trial, however, Madeleine walked free after the jury delivered a controversial not proven verdict. First witness at the trial at Edinburgh High Court was Bridge of Allan postmaster, Charles Neil Rutherford, son of David Rutherford, manager of Keirfield Bleach Works and younger brother of Dr. John Rutherford. Charles founded the first shop in Henderson Street in 1836. As well as being shopkeeper, postmaster and owner of the town's circulating library, he served as the first chemist. Later, two other chemists, Gilbert Farie and Oswald Robertson also established themselves and these rivals forced Ruherford out of business. Farie's shop became Strathallan Pharmacy.

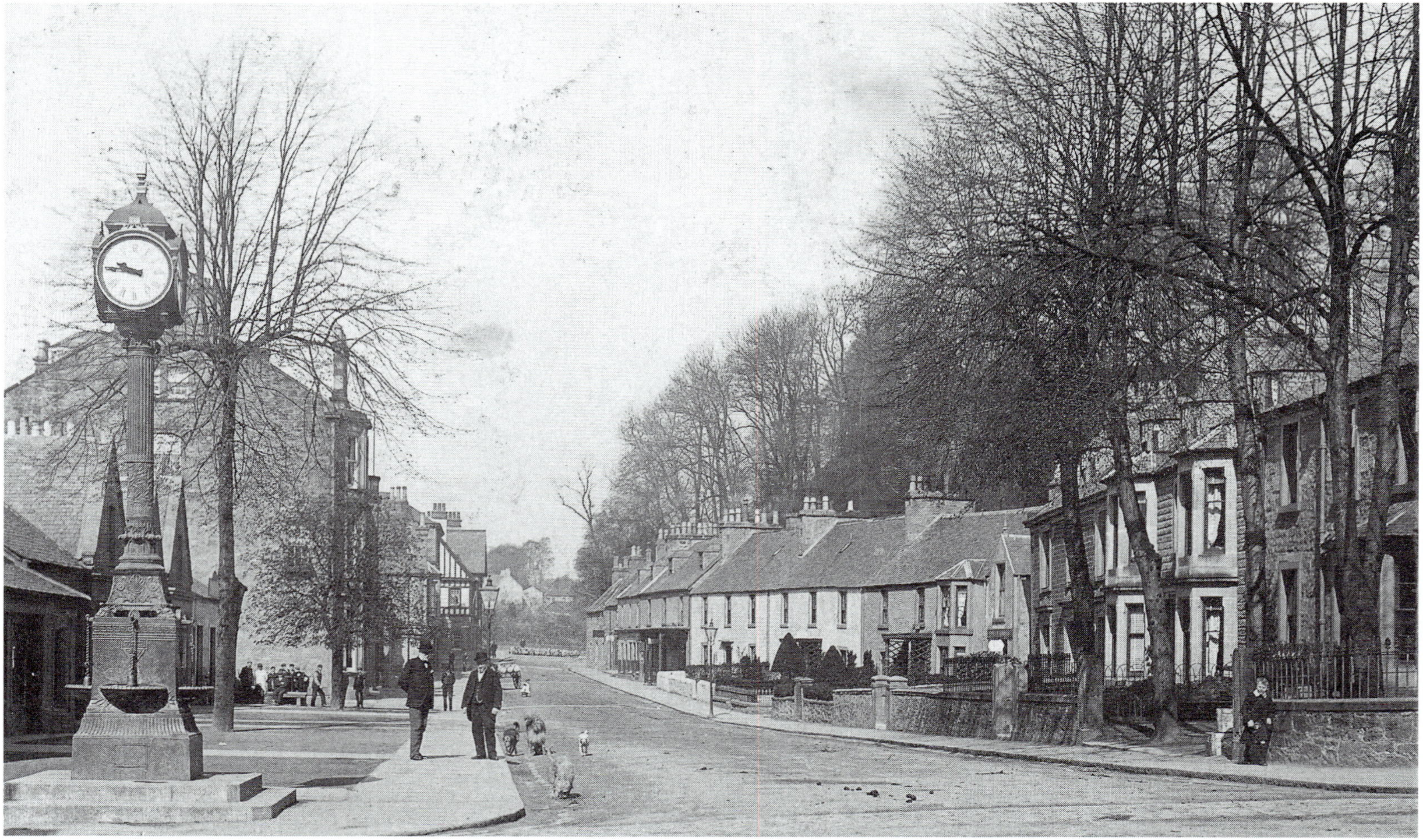

Bridge of Allan's familiar Paterson Clock was erected in 1898 in memory of Dr. Alex Wilkie Paterson, a popular local GP for over half a century who was also local Medical Officer of Health and a Justice of the Peace. He succeeded Dr. John Rutherford, who is remembered for the care he gave patients during a cholera outbreak, despite himself falling ill with the disease. Dr. Paterson did much to promote Bridge of Allan as a spa centre. He also took a great interest in the history of the town and for a time lived at the museum which stood on the north west corner of the Square at this point on Henderson Street. A man of many talents the doctor was also a botanist and horticulturalist, specialising in tropical plants, tree ferns and orchids. The Paterson Clock has three faces and for many years the town councillors struggled with the problem of getting them all to tell the same time.

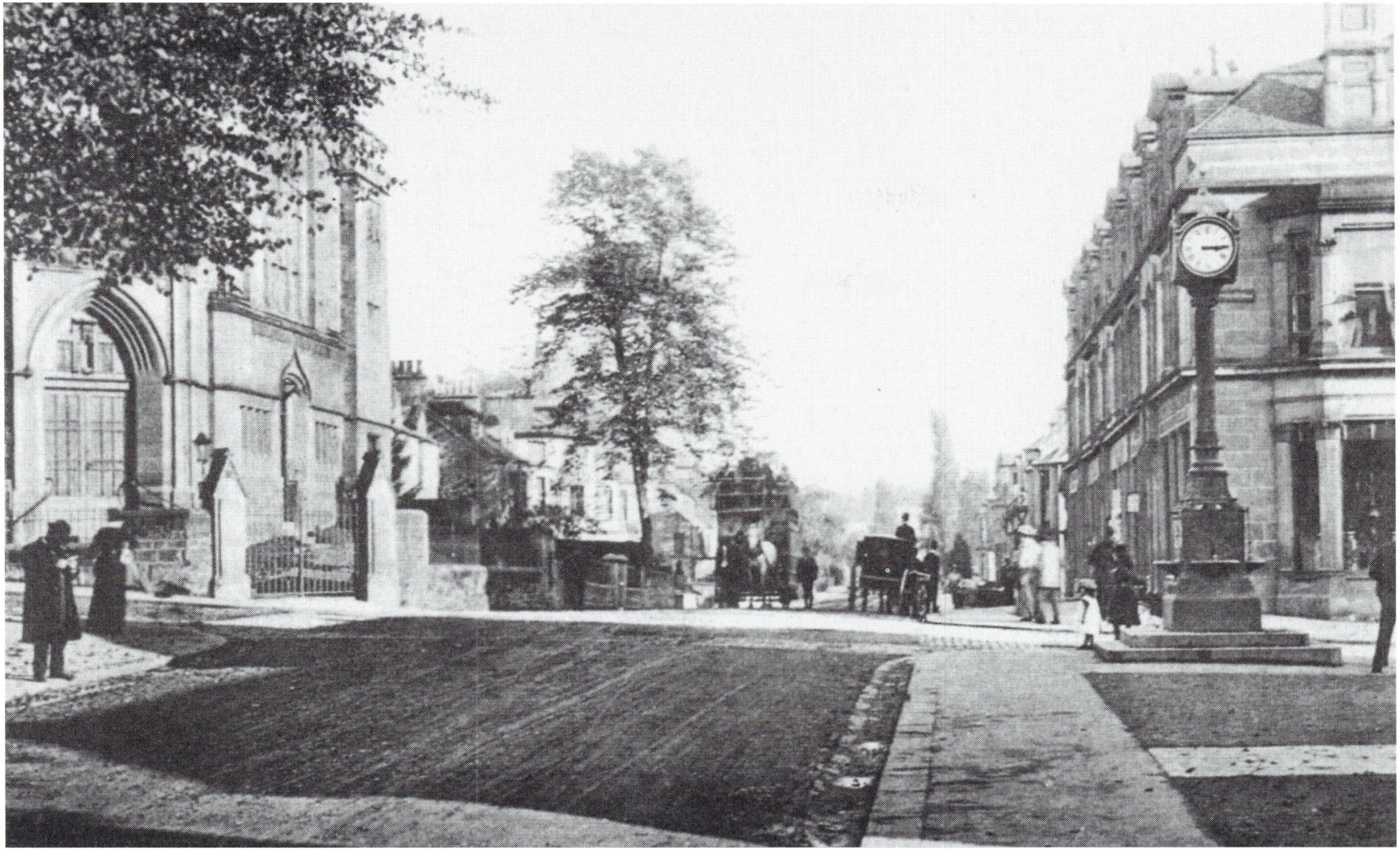

A horse-drawn tram approaches the Tram Terminus circa 1903 with the Queens Hotel on the left. Originally known as Barrs Hotel in Victorian times its guests included famous lighthouse engineer, Thomas Stevenson, his wife and their young son Robert Louis. RLS and his cousin Bob spent a month over Christmas and New Year 1872 in the hotel's first floor north east corner room. Another popular hotel, the Westerton Arms, stands on the corner of Henderson and Union Street. Before becoming a hotel and bar this building housed a reading room. Behind it in what is now the car park was once a tennis court and a bowling green, where Bridge of Allan Bowling Club was founded in 1860. The club moved to its present site at Cornton Green in 1904.

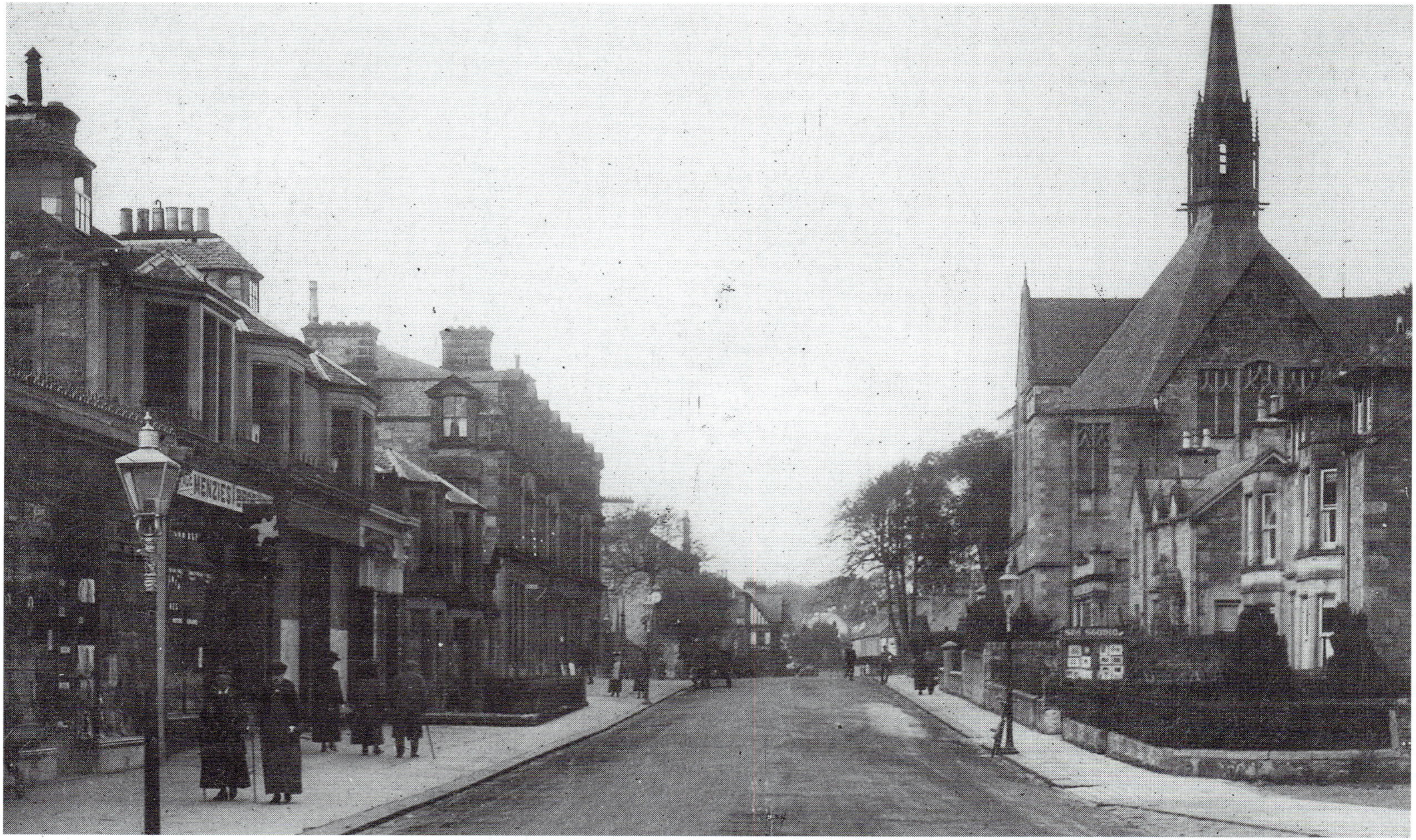

Jutting out into the street in the distance can be seen the former police station. It was situated a short distance before the bridge over the Allan Water and its situation allowed the police officers to keep a close eye on all that was happening in Henderson Street. During the Second World War the by then former police station was brought back into use as headquarters for the town's branch of the ARP and the ARP wardens used to sleep in the former cells. Opposite where it stood is now the location of the Allanwater Cafe. Originally owned by the Togneri family from Italy , it was often referred to as Old Togs and as well as its delicious home made ice cream and fish and chips was famed for serving plates of mushy peas. It is now operated by the Berchelli family (relatives of the Togneris through marriage) who have expanded to include a new gallery restaurant with table license on the first floor.

Two very similar views of Henderson Street the upper view is from 1923. An Alexanders bus passes the Royal Hotel in the 1934 lower view looking west along Henderson Street.

Running parallel with Henderson Street is Keir Street where Cleopatra's Garden is situated. Local laird, Sir James Alexander of Westerton, a noted antiquarian, played a large role in bringing Cleopatra's Needle to Britain and local tradition insists that at one point he intended raising it on this site, rather than on the Embankment overlooking the Thames, where it was eventually sited. There is no written proof for this claim and in the end the little garden in Bridge of Allan was utilised instead for the planting of a tree to commemorate Queen Victoria's Diamond Jubilee in 1897.

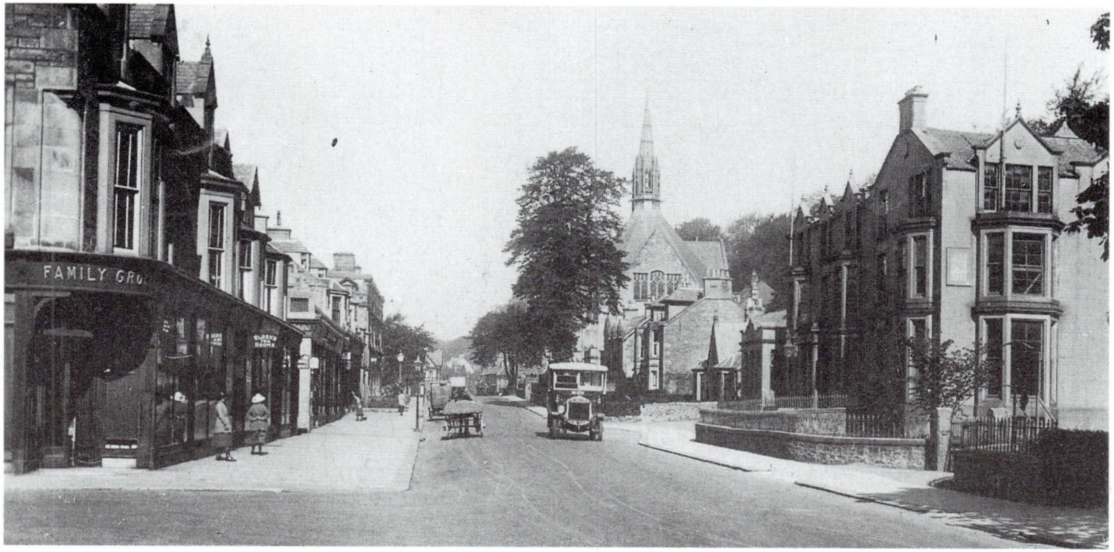

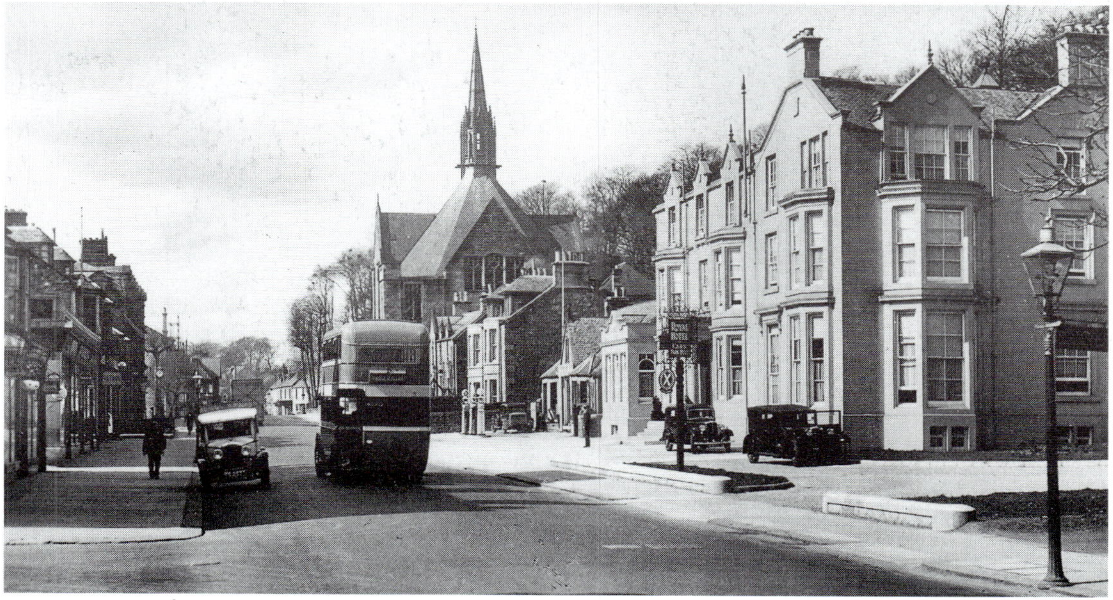

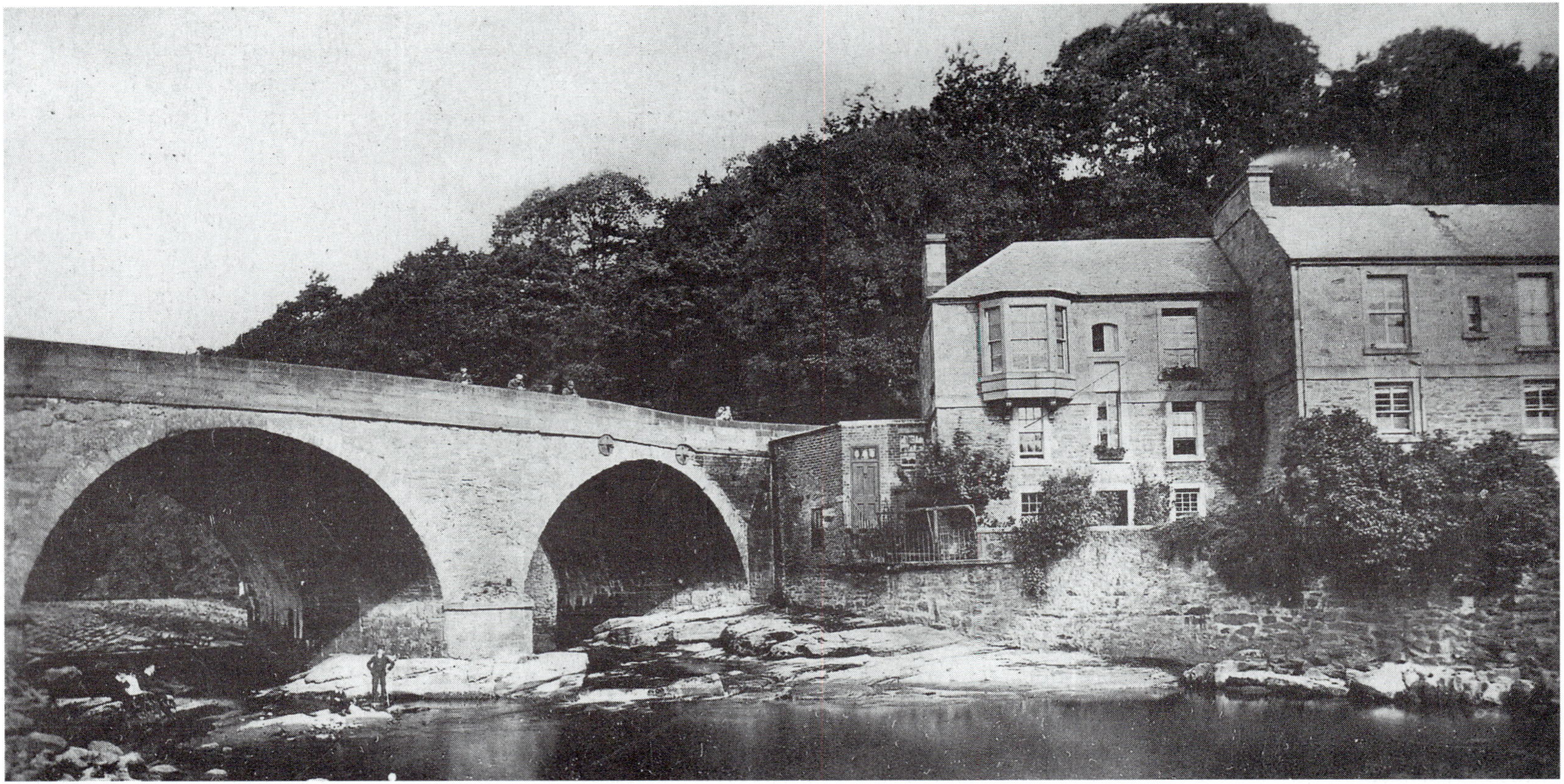

The original bridge over the Allan Water was built in 1520 to replace the dangerous ford which had until then been the only way to cross the river at this point. The old bridge was altered in 1842 to enable it to bear heavier loads. With an awkward bend at the Henderson Street end causing more and more traffic delays, the old bridge remained the only way to cross the river until it was finally replaced by the present bridge in 1958. Plans for this had been drawn up as early as the 1930s but were delayed by the Second World War and subsequent post-war shortages of building materials. When work on the reinforced concrete span began in the mid-1950s steel was still in very short supply and had supplies had to be imported from Poland. To prevent the flow of traffic on this very important route to the north (as it was at the time, before the M9 motorway) from being interrupted, the new bridge was built in two halves. The first vehicles were permitted to travel over the carriageway on one side of the bridge in 1957. A small section of parapet and the remains of the piers of the old bridge can still be glimpsed in the waters below the new bridge. In the days of horse-drawn traffic there was a change house at the end of the bridge at the west end of Henderson Street. This building rose from the level of the river to the level of the bridge and was where that horses were changed to enable the mail coaches to maintain their advertised speed and journey times between Edinburgh, Stirling, Perth and the north of Scotland. At the bridge level also stood the toll house where for decades all vehicles had to stop and pay at the toll bar in order to proceed further.

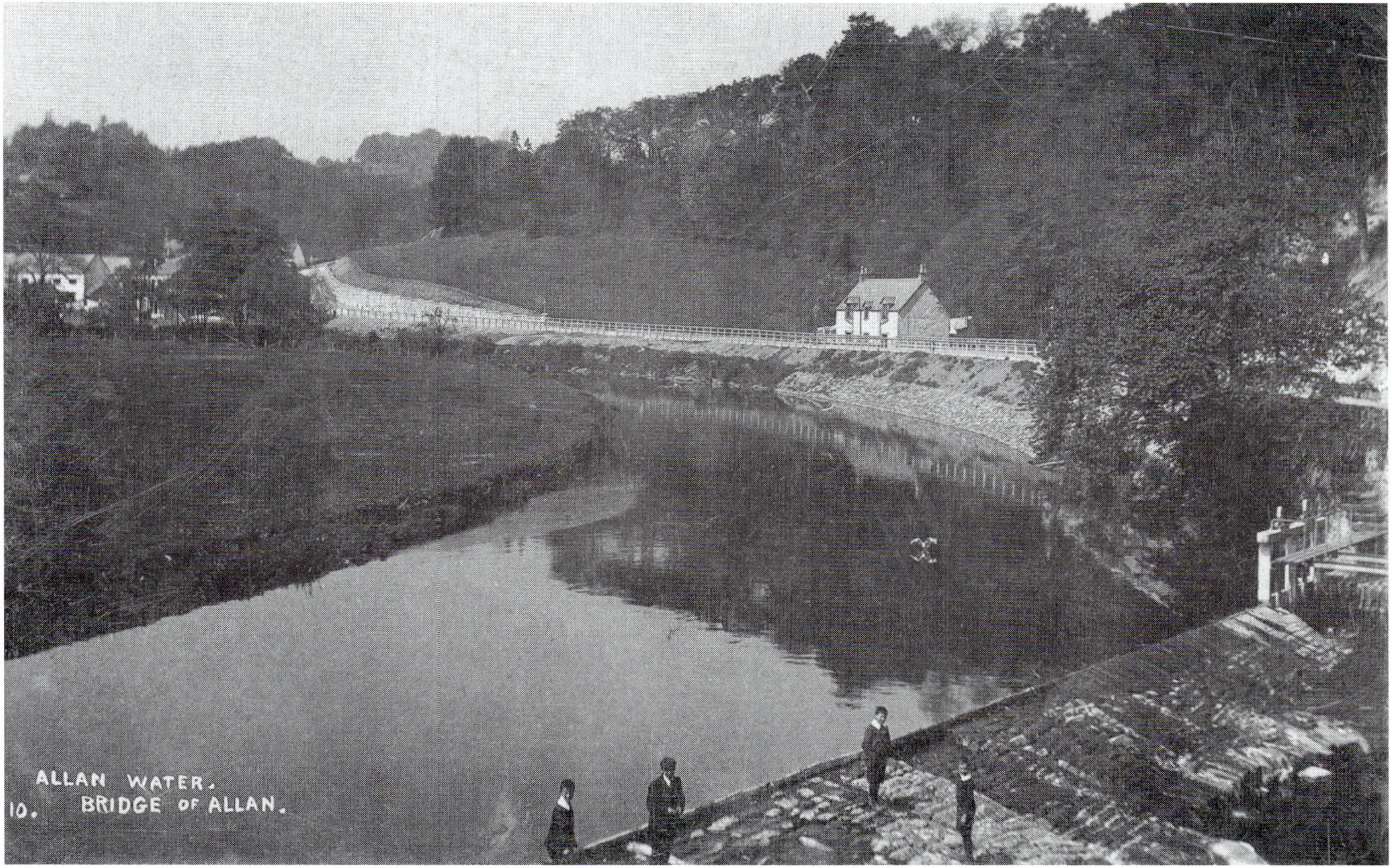

Smartly uniformed schoolboys wearing white starched Eton collars are standing on the apron of the weir to add period interest to this shot of the Allan Water. Halfway up stream along Blairforkie Drive can be seen Salisbury Cottage, now long demolished.

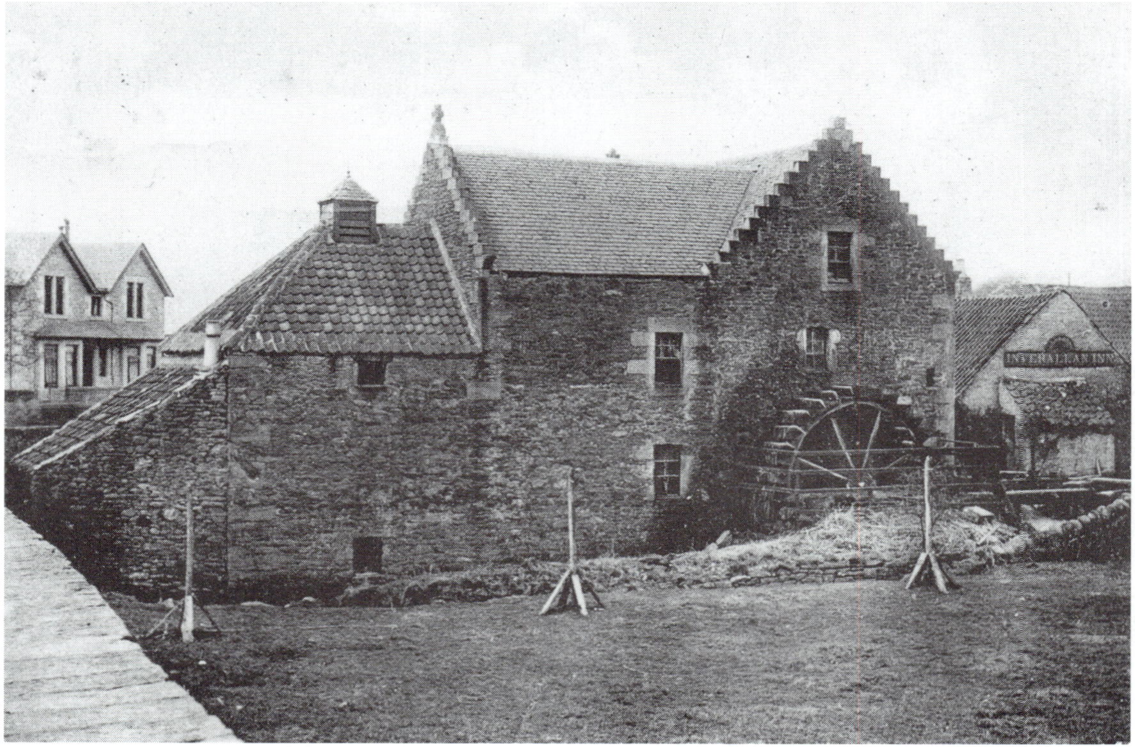

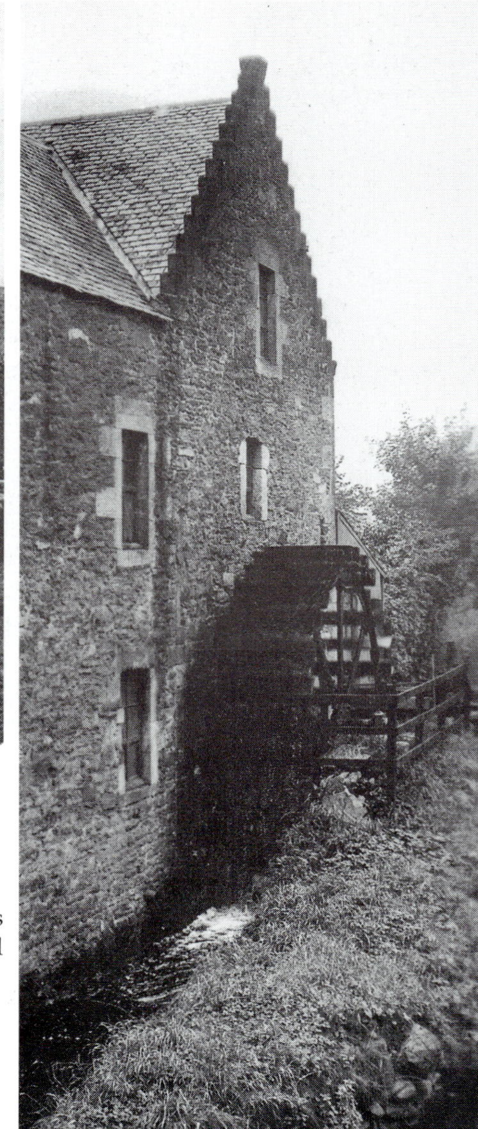

The old Inverallan Meal Mill still stands on the banks of the Allan Water. Situated in Inverallan Road, it is now the offices of D M H Baird . Although the water wheel has been preserved the mill lade has been infilled and returned to nature. Nearby stands the Bridge Inn, one of Bridge of Allan's oldest drinking howffs.

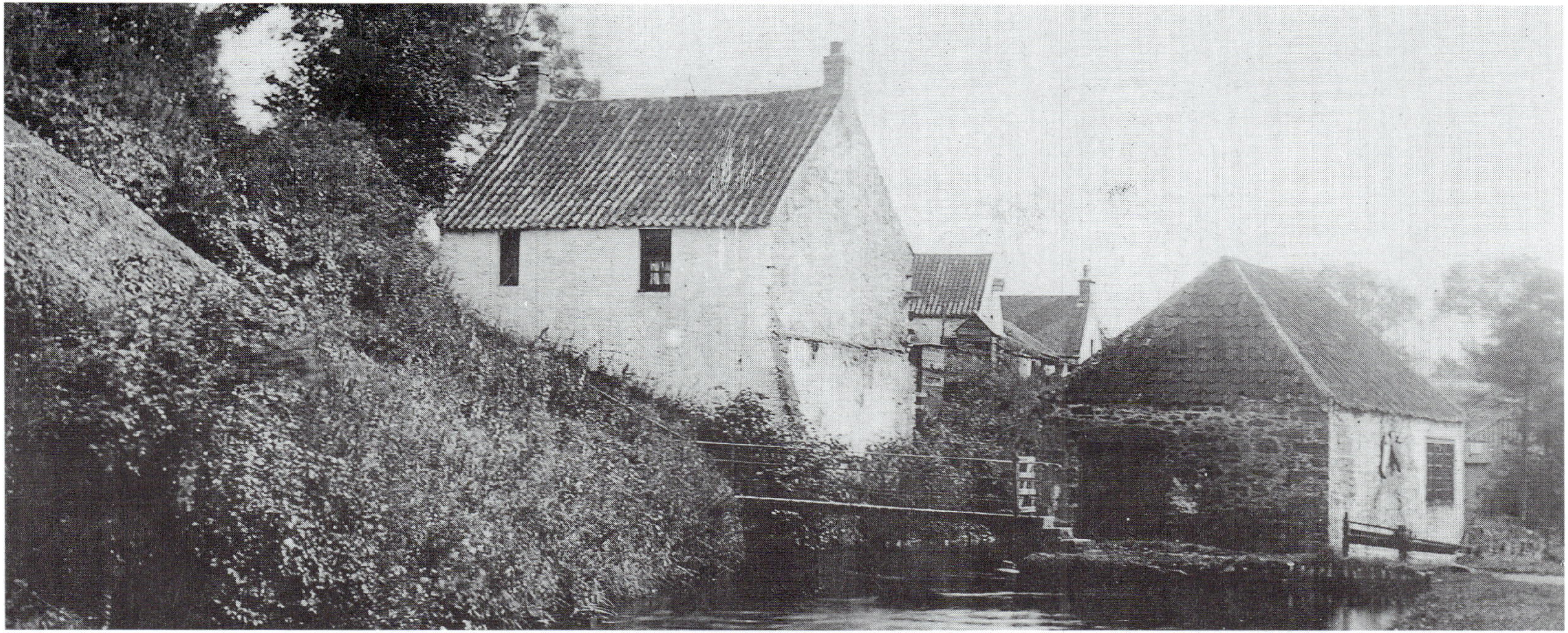

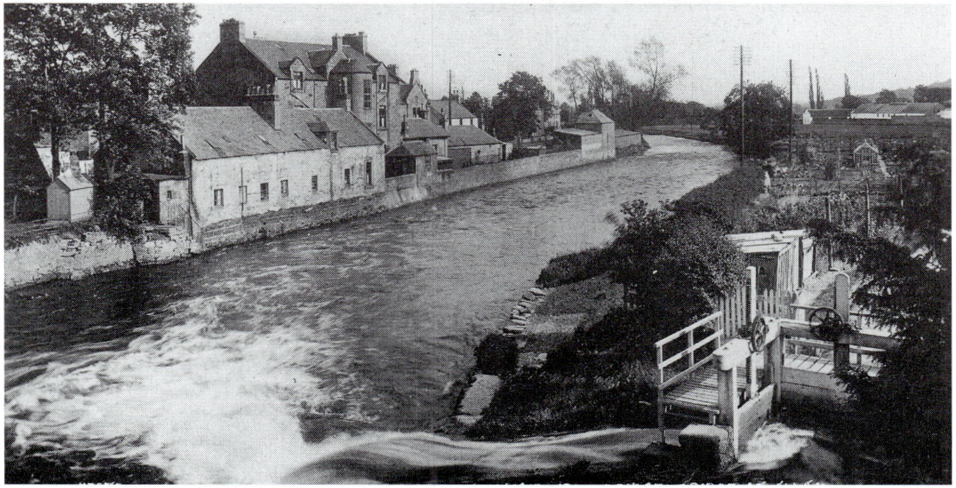

Two views connected to the operation of the old meal mill. The top one is described as showing the Mill Lock, where the water for the lade which powered the big wheel was drawn from the Allan Water, while the one below shows where the water from the lade re-entered the river near Keirfield Farm.

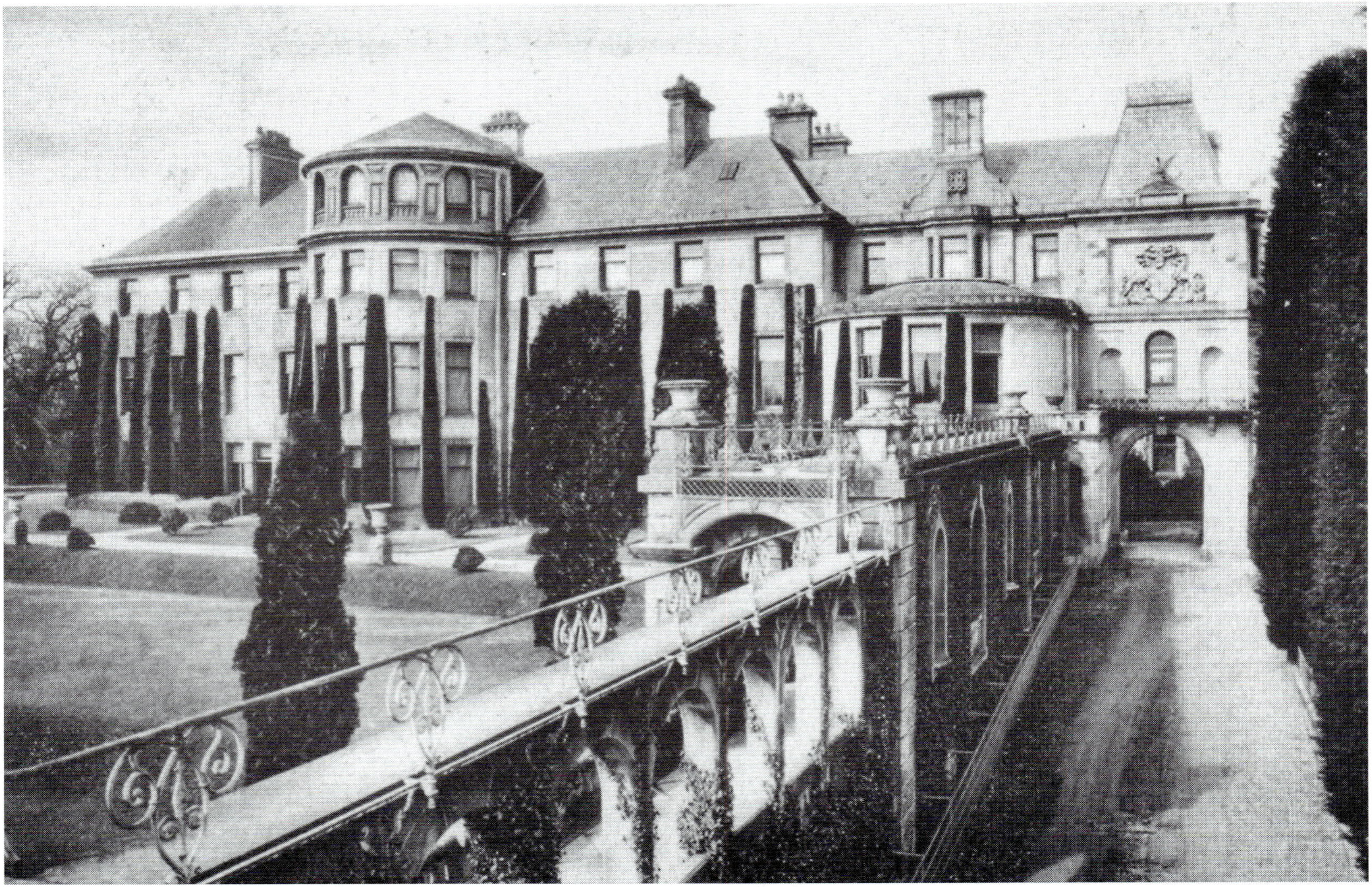

The magnificent Keir House and its estate lie to the north of the town near the site of the large roundabout at the northern end of the M9 motorway and was originally home to the Stirling family. To increase their privacy they moved the hamlet of Lecropt off their land so that now only Lecropt Parish Church remains, separated from its burial yard by the main road.

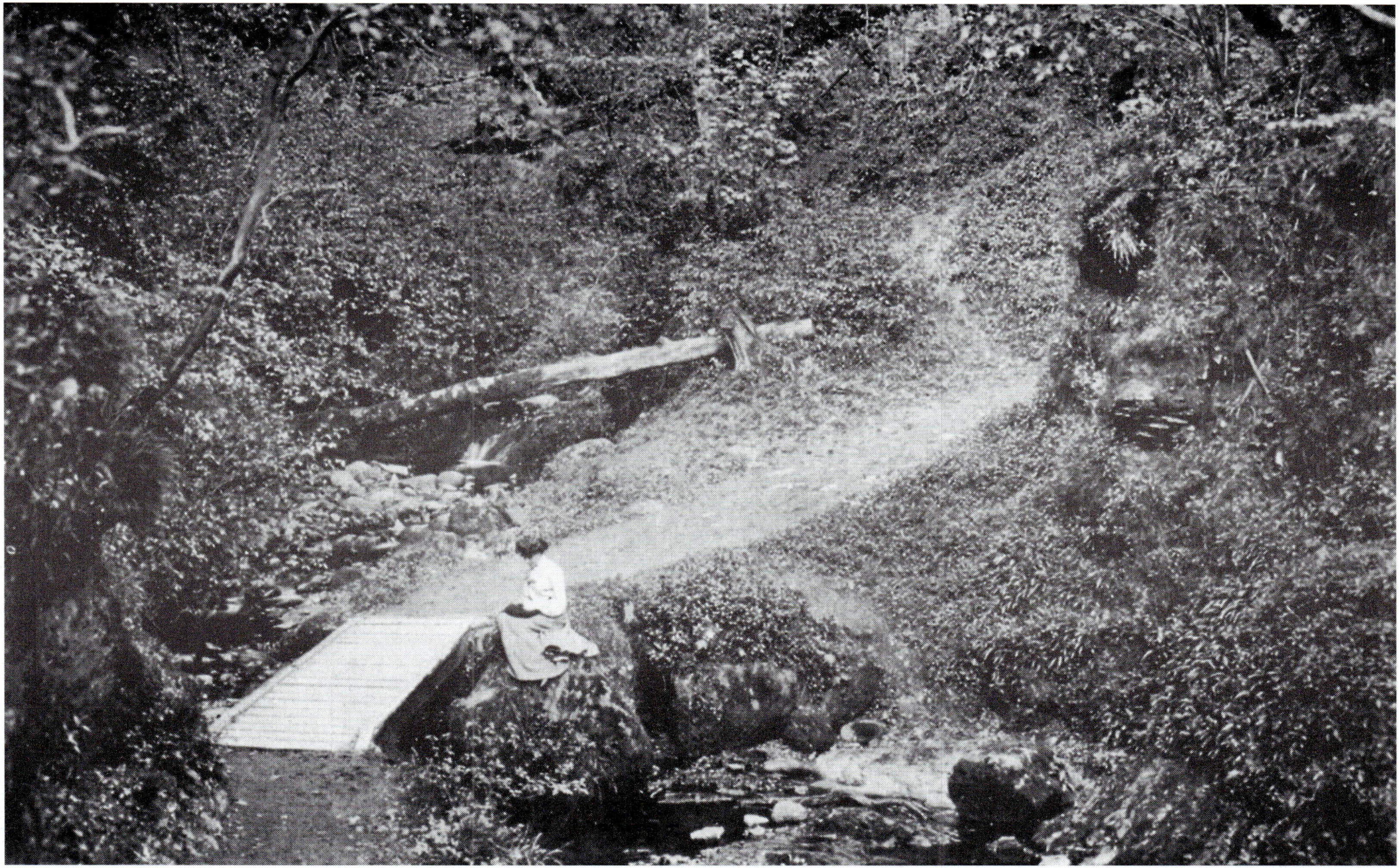

Wharry Glen is one of many local beauty spots on the slopes of the surrounding Ochil Hills. The pronunciation of Ochil often proves difficult for visitors; one story has an American who asked the receptionist at the Royal Hotel how long it would take him "to climb to the summit of the O C Hills".

The bridge in the picture was washed away and so was its successor, but the modern replacement has survived, making this a popular rural walk. The water from the Wharry Burn feeds into Airthrey Loch in the grounds of the University of Stirling.

Airthrey Castle stands to the east of town in the centre of Stirling University campus. Originally the home of the Haldane family, this large and impressive castle was not designed by Robert Adam as is sometimes claimed, but Adam did work to improve its appearance. The Airthrey Estate was bought by Sir Robert Abercromby in 1798 and he did much to encourage the development of Bridge of Allan as a spa town by sending specimens of the water from the copper mine to be analysed in Glasgow in 1820. The castle was extended in 1889. Before being taken over by the university in 1966, it served for many years as a maternity hospital for expectant mothers from a large part of the west of Scotland.

Airthrey Castle overlooks an artificial loch, the scene of a tragedy in 1901 when 26 year old Fred Pullar, son of the well-known owners of the Bridge of Allan Bleach Works, was drowned while trying to rescue a young woman who had gone through the ice while skating on its frozen surface.

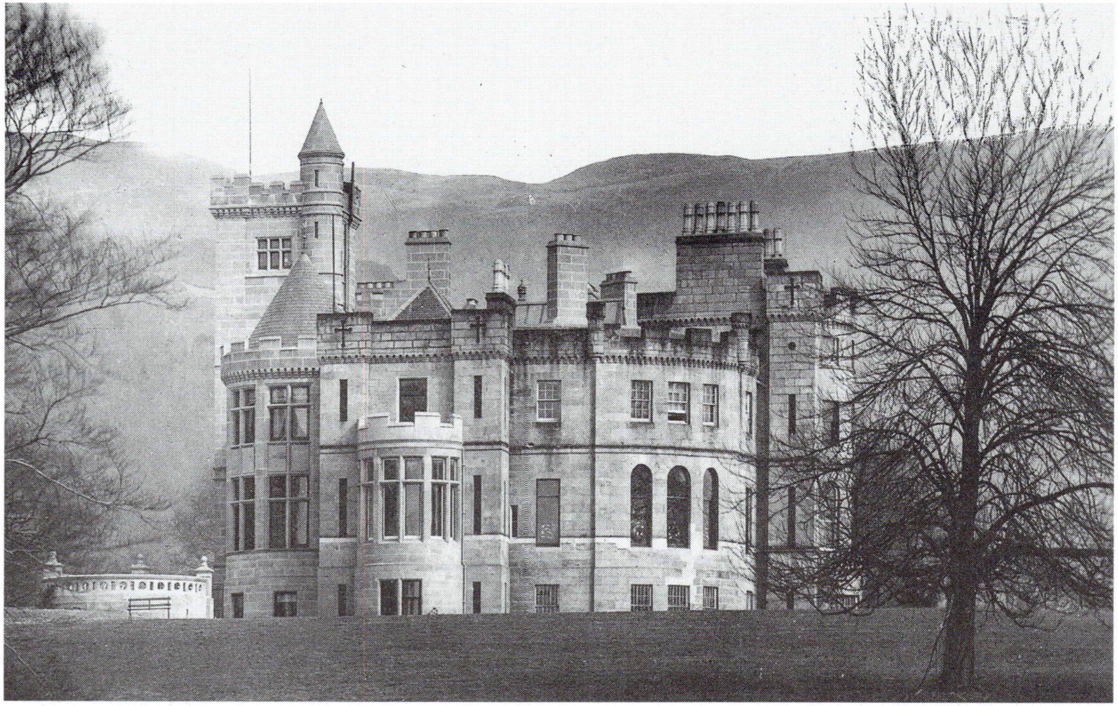

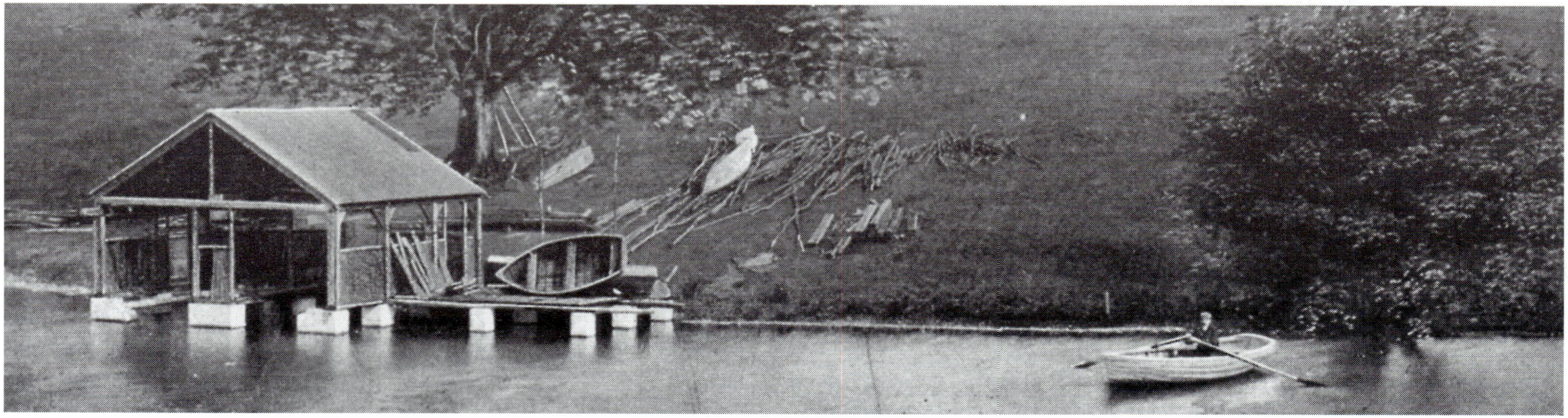

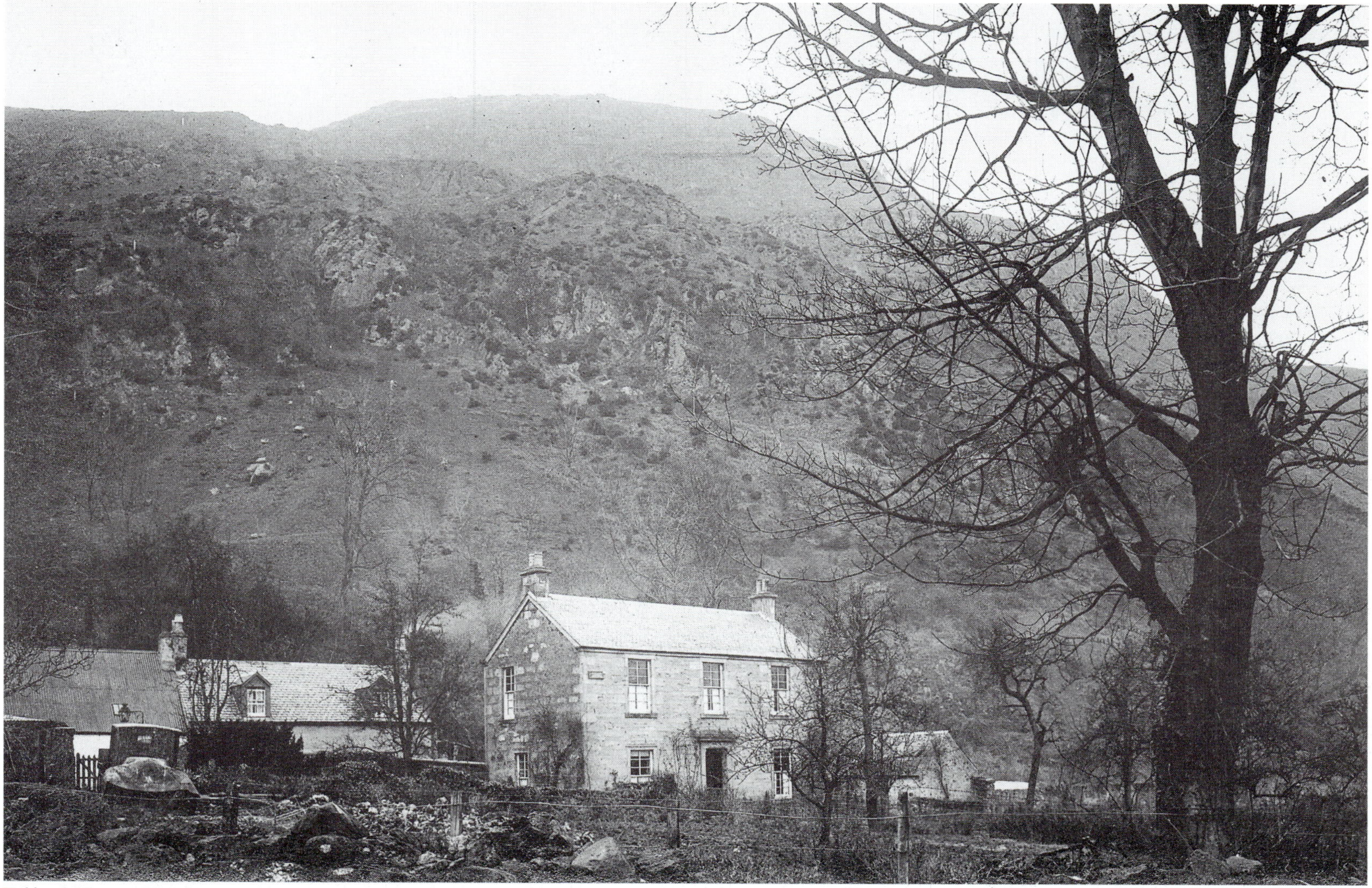

Telford House, Blairlogie, takes its name from the family who originally feued the plot of land on which it stands from the owners of Blairlogie Castle. The Telfords were firstly joiners, but later in the 19th century, a member of the family became one of the first bankers in Stirling. Overlooked by the Ochil Hills, Telford House, is one of the most attractive houses in Blairlogie. It was built on a site previously occupied by single-storey thatched cottages.

The ruins of the original Old Kirk of Logie and its graveyard. The kirk was built around 1400 and dedicated to St.Serf. Many of the tombstones date from the 17th and 18th centuries. The Old Kirk was replaced by the present Logie Kirk in 1805. Nearby is the Witches Crag where the witches of Logie are reputed to have met the Devil. The Witches Crag is sometimes also known as the Carlie Craig, this being a corruption of Carlin , the old Scottish word for witch (see also page 47).

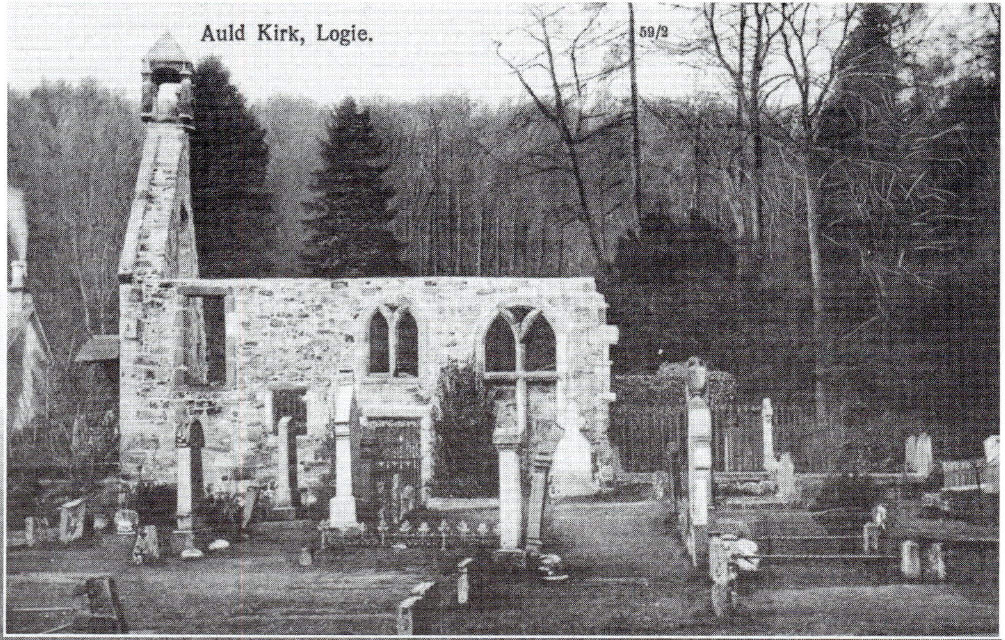

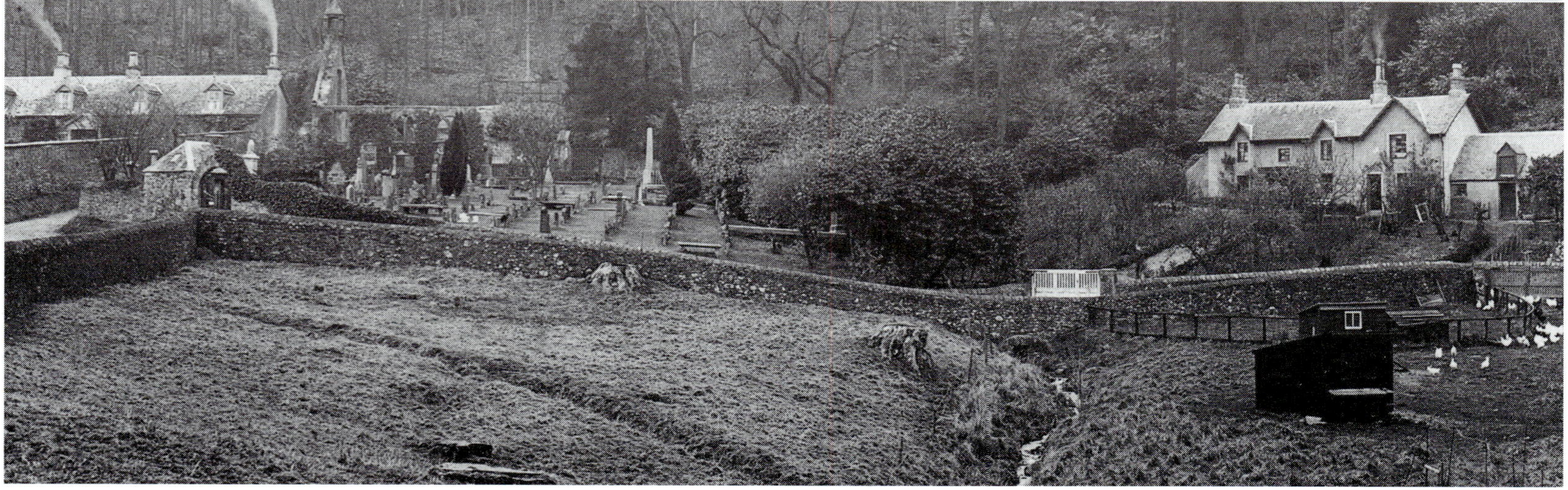

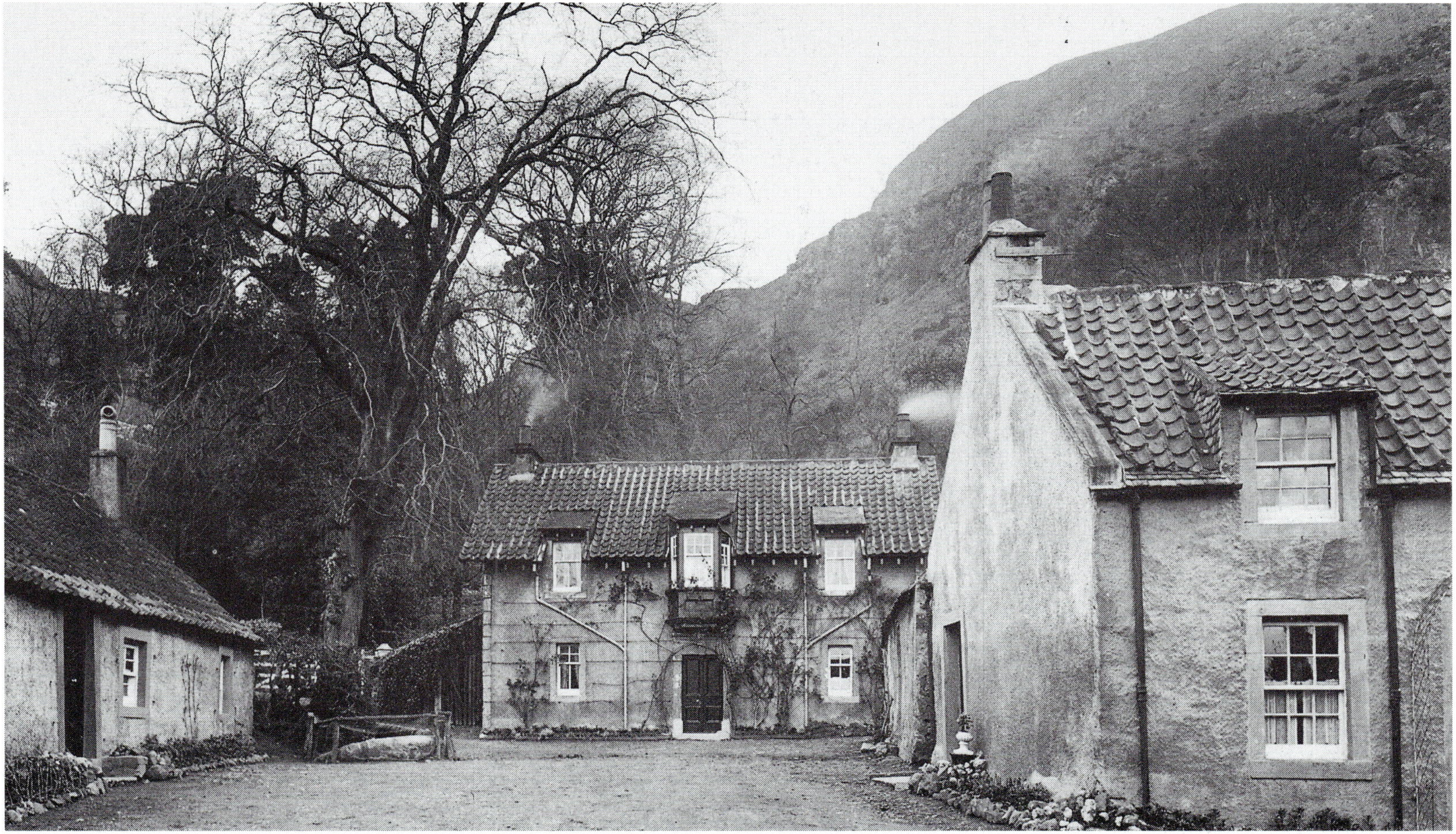

The castle entrance and area known as The Square in front of it lie at the heart of Blairlogie. In this picturesque scene Ivy Cottage is to the left , Montana in the centre and Hillside to the right. For many years Ivy Cottage was the home of the gardener for Blairlogie Castle estate and he is given credit for having planted the Montana Clematis plant from which the house in the middle derives its unusual name. At one time the main road between Stirling and Kinross and the north passed through The Square and a carved stone in the wall of Montana depicting the number 4 with forked endings to its upright leg and cross bar, indicates that this used to be the setting for a regular wool market. The date stone on Montana suggests that it was built in 1765 and the present owners, George and Rae McIntosh, during renovations have come upon square headed clout nails, which are indicative of its 18th century origins, despite doubt being cast upon these by an architectural guide.

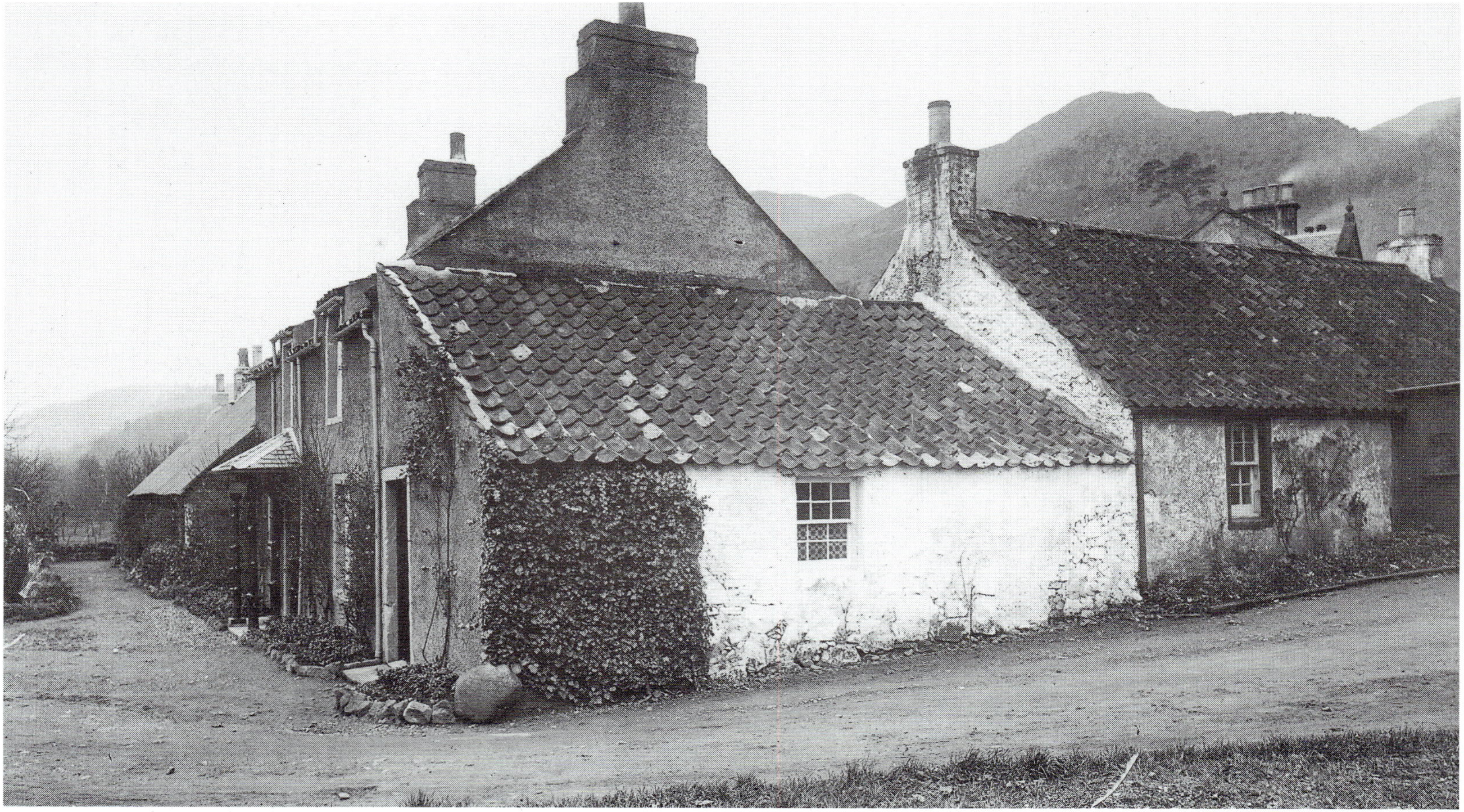

Kirklea is one of the most attractive of the old cottages in Blairlogie. A wedding lintel or juncture stone, now resited above the entrance to the cottage's garage, shows that it was originally built by Alexander Williamson and his wife. The cottage is now occupied by writer and local historian Robin Kelsall whose actor father, Moultrie, originally purchased it. Named Kirklea, it does indeed nestle in the shelter of the former Blairlogie United Free Kirk, which stands opposite. It now incorporates what was originally a separate cottage, Burnside, seen here against the backdrop of the Ochil Hills. Beyond Kirklea on the left can be glimpsed three little thatched cottages. Now demolished, they were rather grandly known as Victoria Place, named after Britain's longest reigning monarch. Amongst Victoria Places residents were a tailor and a soutar or shoe maker, in the days when Blairlogie was a self-sufficient little hamlet. Kirklea was one of the first houses, not only in Blairlogie but in the whole of the Hillfoots, to be connected by telephone. Its number was originally Menstrie 3.

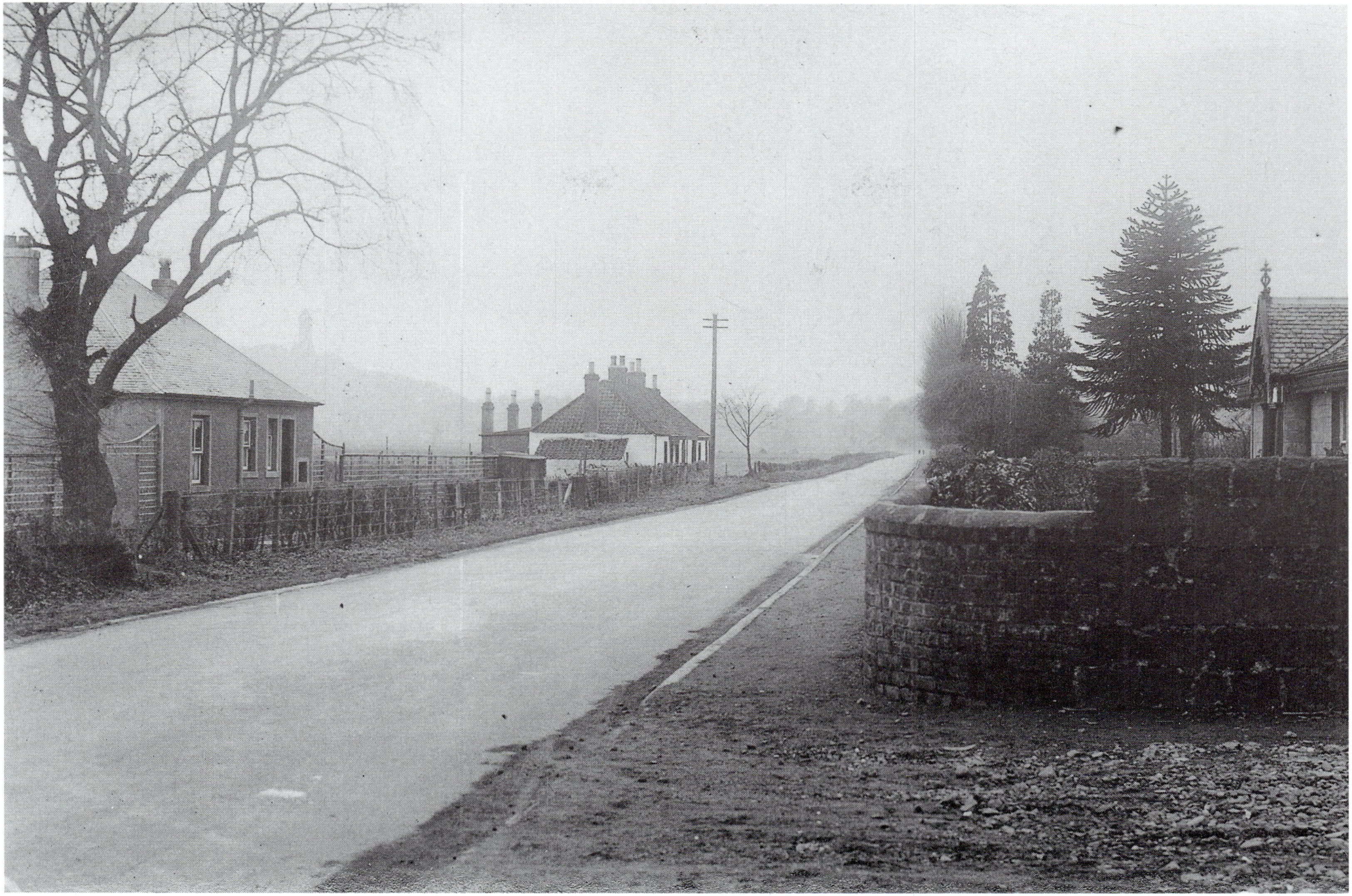

A deserted Hillfoot Road photographed in the late 1920s. The house beside the tree on the left is now known as Caradona, but was for many decades called San Julien. Blairlogie's original post office was housed in the farm cottages also seen on the left.

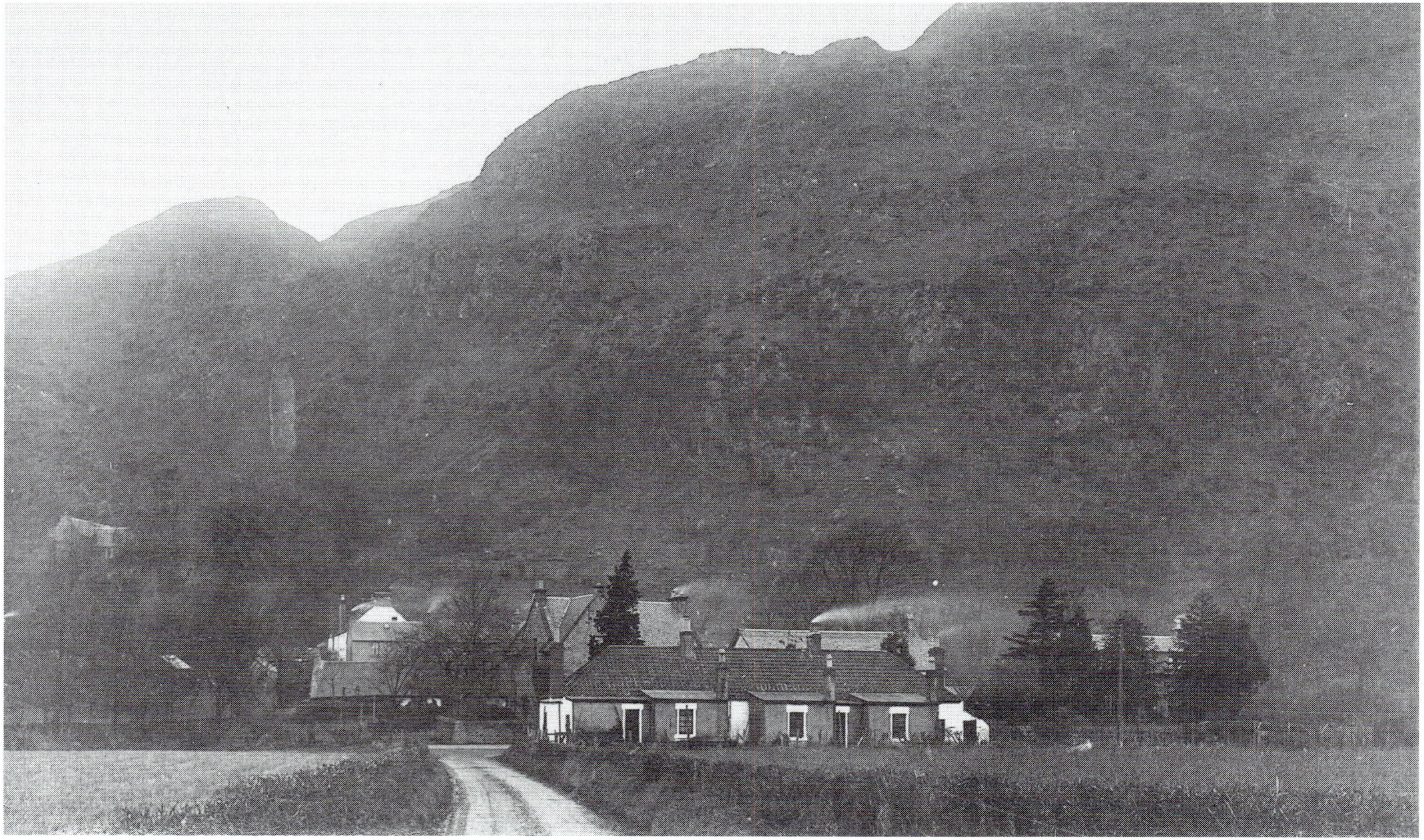

Blairlogie village lies tucked below the Ochil Hills, highest of which is Dumyat, seen here in the background. Beyond the farm cottages (as seen in the previous picture) the roofs of the former United Free Church and its manse can be glimpsed. The manse rivalled the church in size and was a 19th century replacement for an earlier smaller house, dating like the church from 1761. The original 18th century Seceder building was destroyed by fire in 1845 and rebuilt along the same lines in 1847. The exterior is unadorned apart from a small belfry above the west gable. Restoration work in the 1970s revealed evidence that there was originally an exterior stone stairway leading to the balcony on the north side of the building. Its congregation now worships in what was formerly the church hall in the neighbouring Hillfoots village of Menstrie.

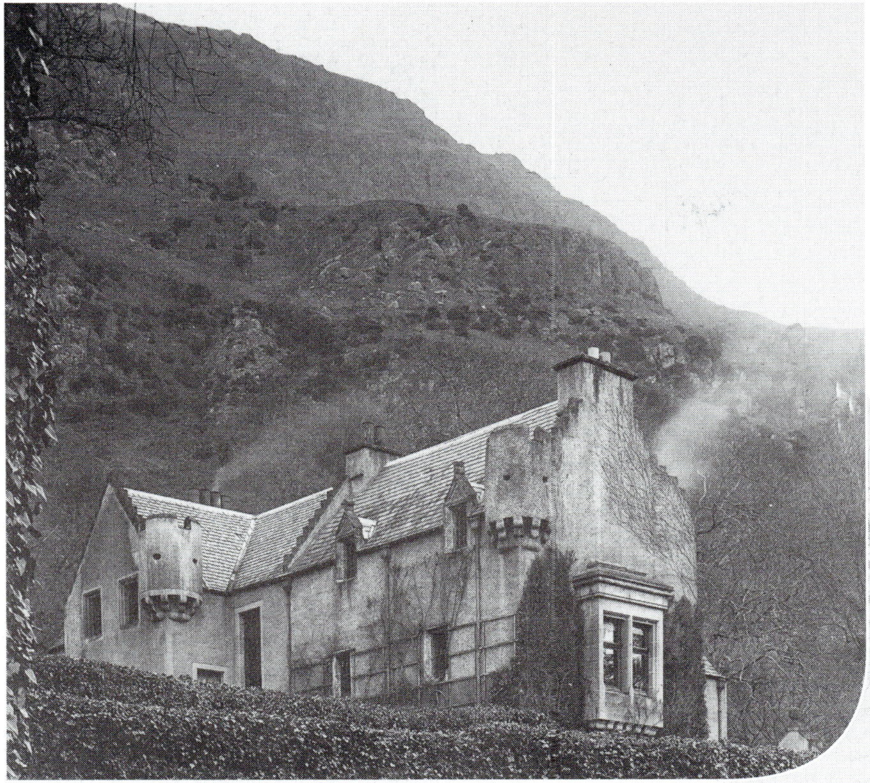

Blairlogie Castle is a small tower house and dates from 1546, with the east wing added in 1582. A carved stone above one of its dormer windows is carved with the letters A.S. and E. H., its first owners Alexander Spittal and his wife Elizabeth Hay. The castle remained in the hands of the Spittal family for over two hundred years until 1767. A later owner cut the name down and called it simply The Blair. The reason for this change , so the story goes, was that he was convinced that when he gave his address for the delivery of his groceries as a castle, he was always charged extra. Tradition maintains that there is a secret room in the castle.

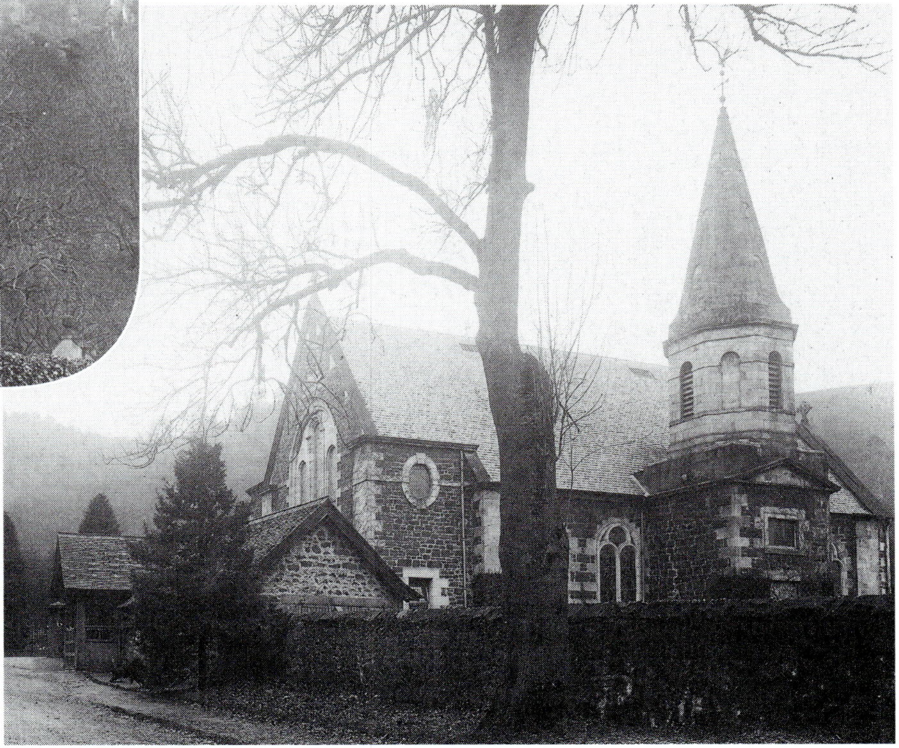

The present Logie Kirk, with its pedimented square tower surmounted by a distinctive octagonal belfry, was erected in 1805. Around the chancel and on the pulpit, fourteen carved oak panels show scenes from the Bible. Logie church is open to visitors under The Churches to Visit in Scotland scheme. In Bridge of Allan Holy Trinity and St. Saviour's are both open to visitors under the scheme. The churches each have fine examples of stained glass and former is of particular interest because the furnishings of its chancel were designed by Charles Rennie Mackintosh.

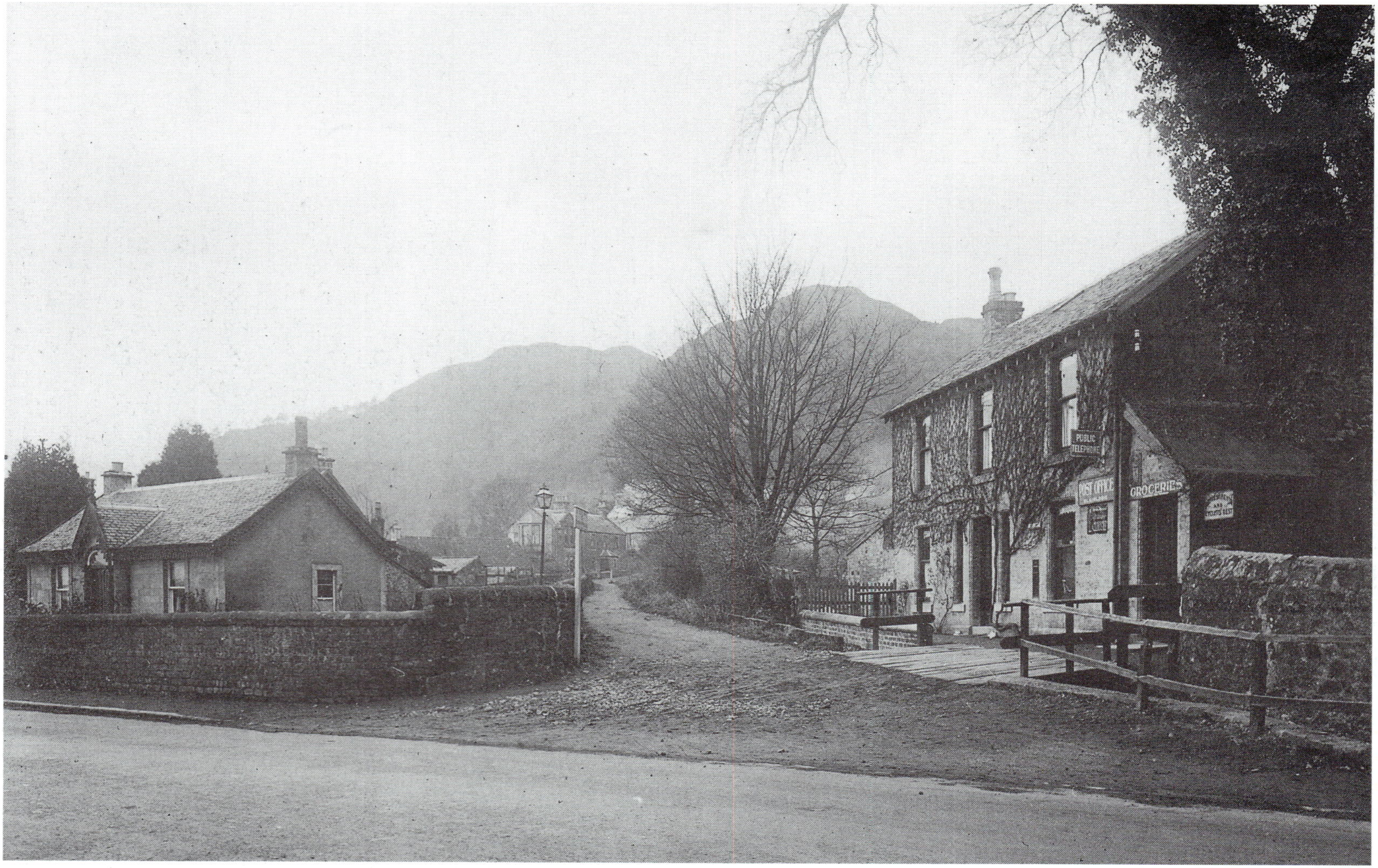

This view shows Nethercraig, which for many years housed the village post office. After it closed it was converted into the very popular Puddleduck Tea Room, a name derived form the little duck pond in the garden. Nethercraig is once again a private house, but Blairlogie is still a popular venue for afternoon teas and morning coffees and light lunches as local farmer John Logan has diversified from his agricultural roots by opening part of his steading at Blairmains as the Coffee Bothy. John is cousin of Scottish rugby internationalist, Kenny Logan, who farms neighbouring Powis Mains.